I0494748

A/CLINK PRESENTS:

#MEBEEPS

LAYOUT BY: AARON COLEMAN

ARTWORK © 2016 BY: AARON COLEMAN

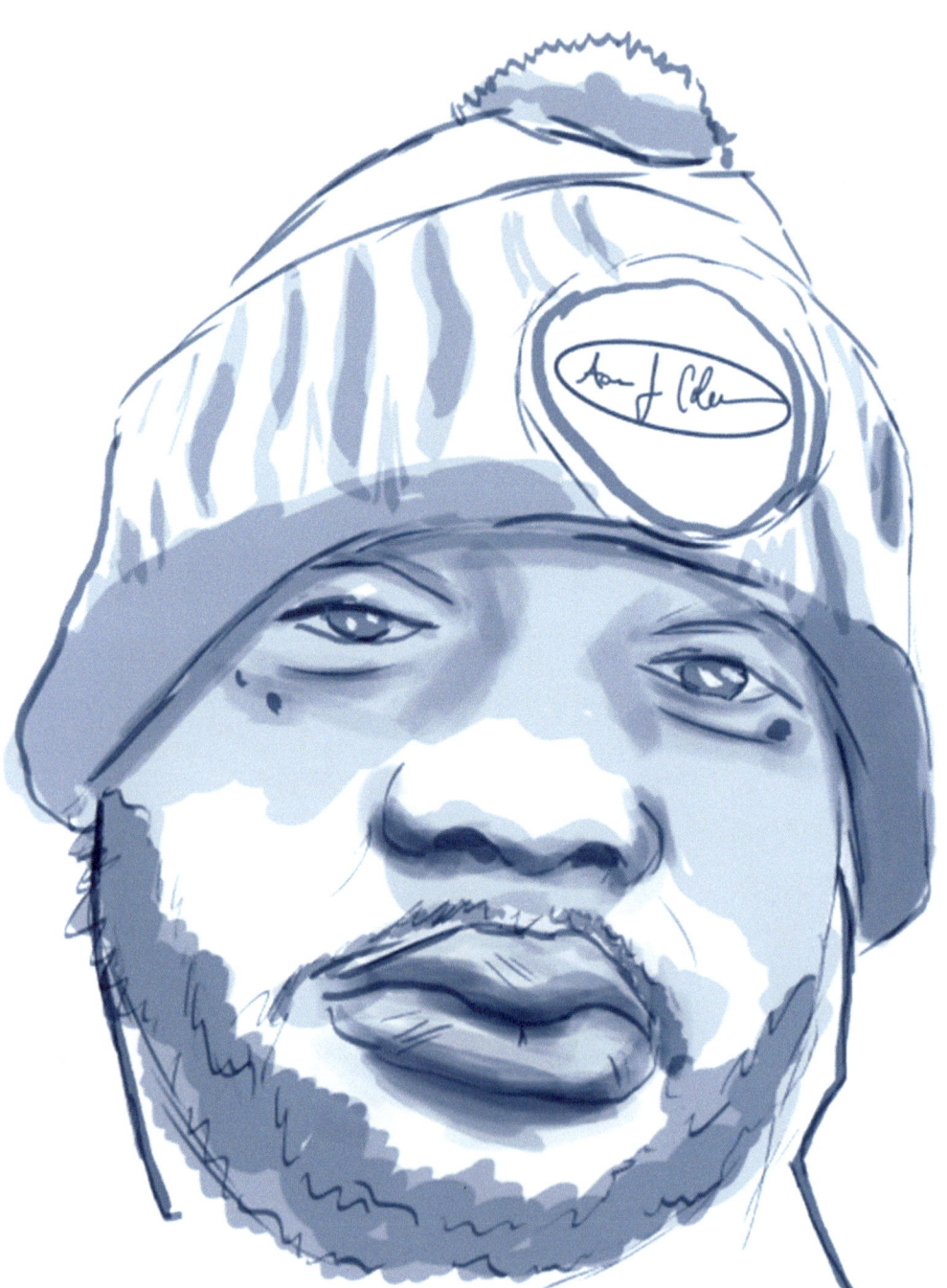

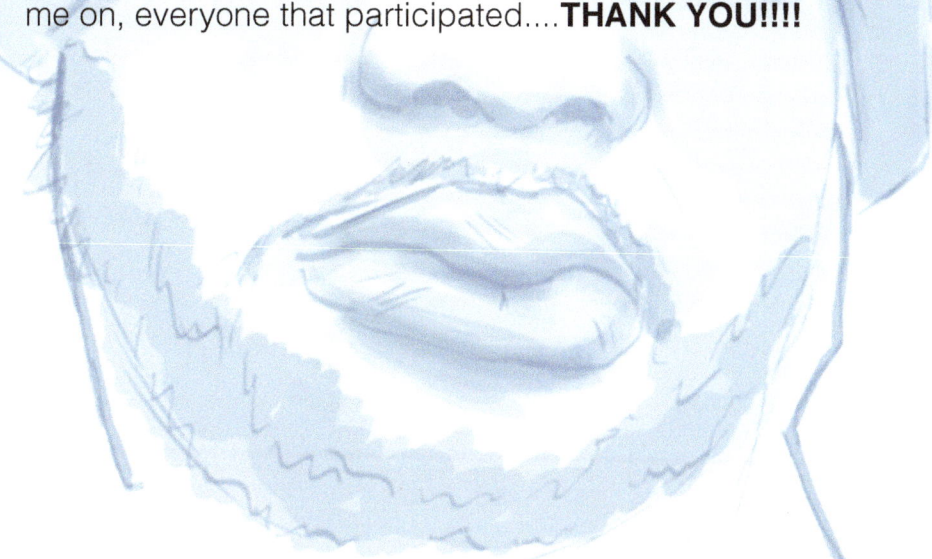

Where to start? What or who are "webpeeps". I define it as a collective of friendly, passionate, creative and all around cool people I have met, or have interactions with via the internet. The idea stemmed from a two sketches I did in early 2015, and it grew into this. Pretty cool, right? (rhetorical if you think it isn't)

This book took on many forms in the beginning, but after several conversations with myself and those who support my goals, this is what was produced. This book was also done as a challenge to myself. I wanted to draw more. Get better at drawing. Something I love doing, but in all honesty, don't do enough of.

So to everyone that suggested I do this, everyone that cheered me on, everyone that participated....**THANK YOU!!!!**

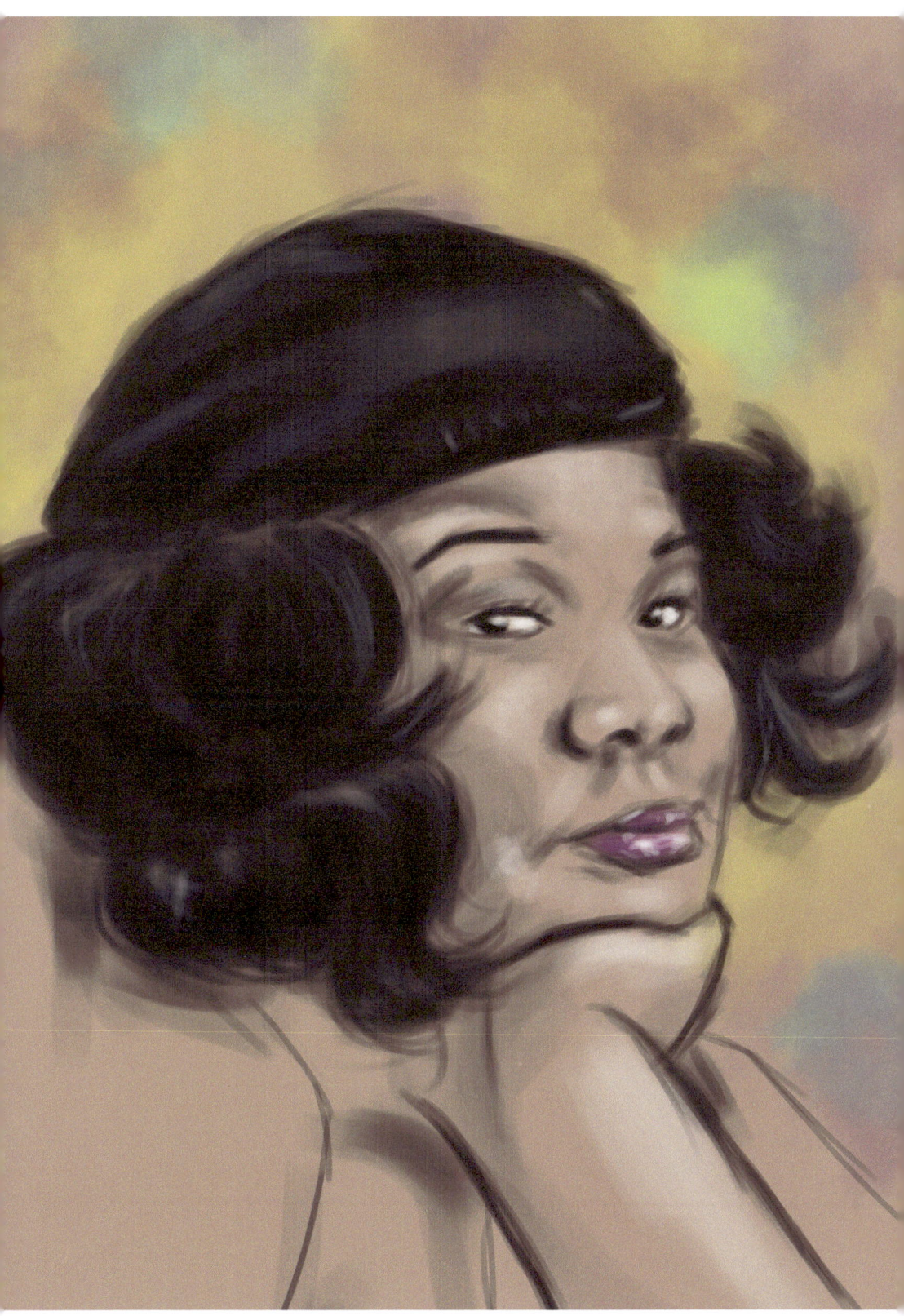

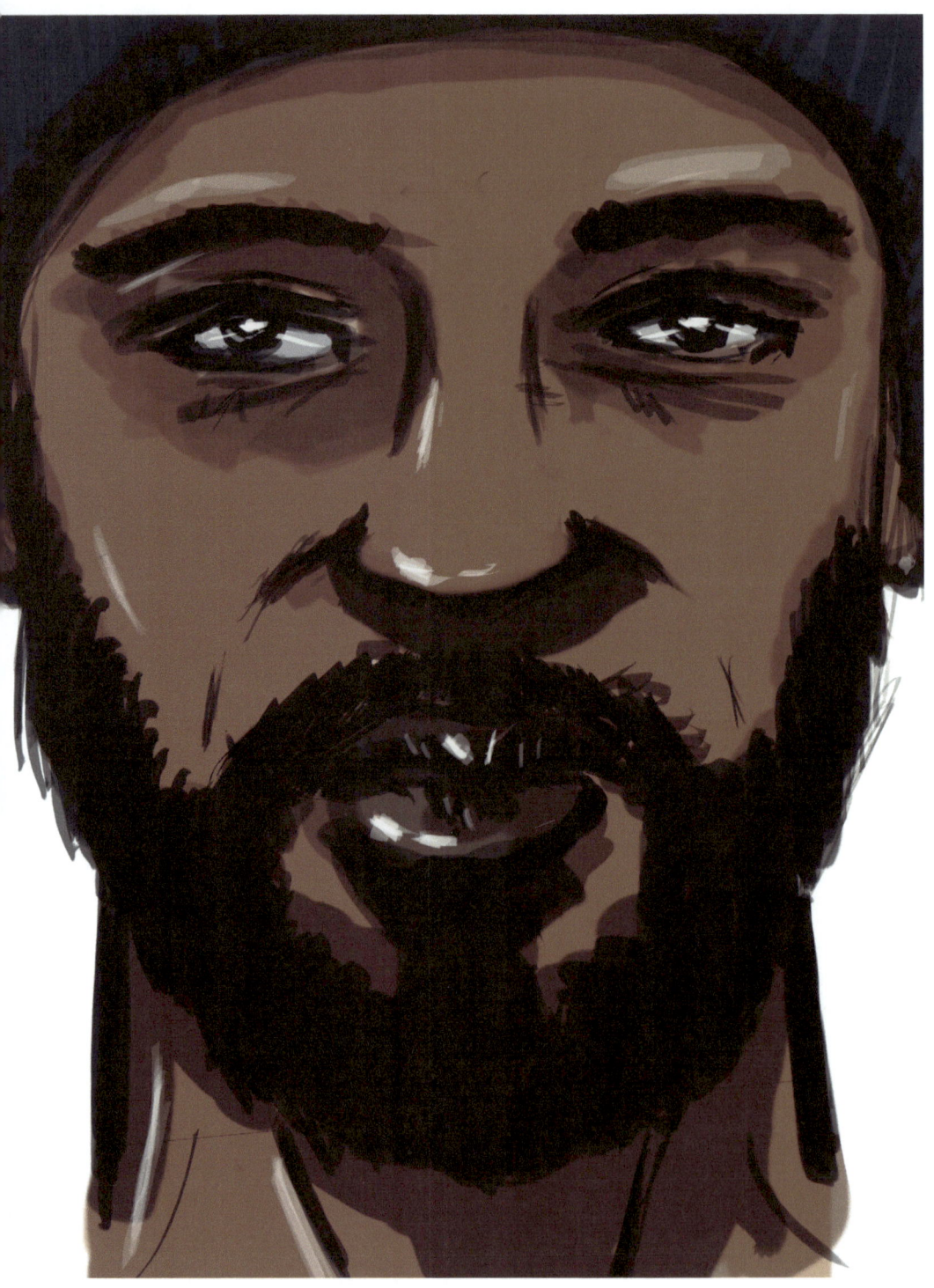

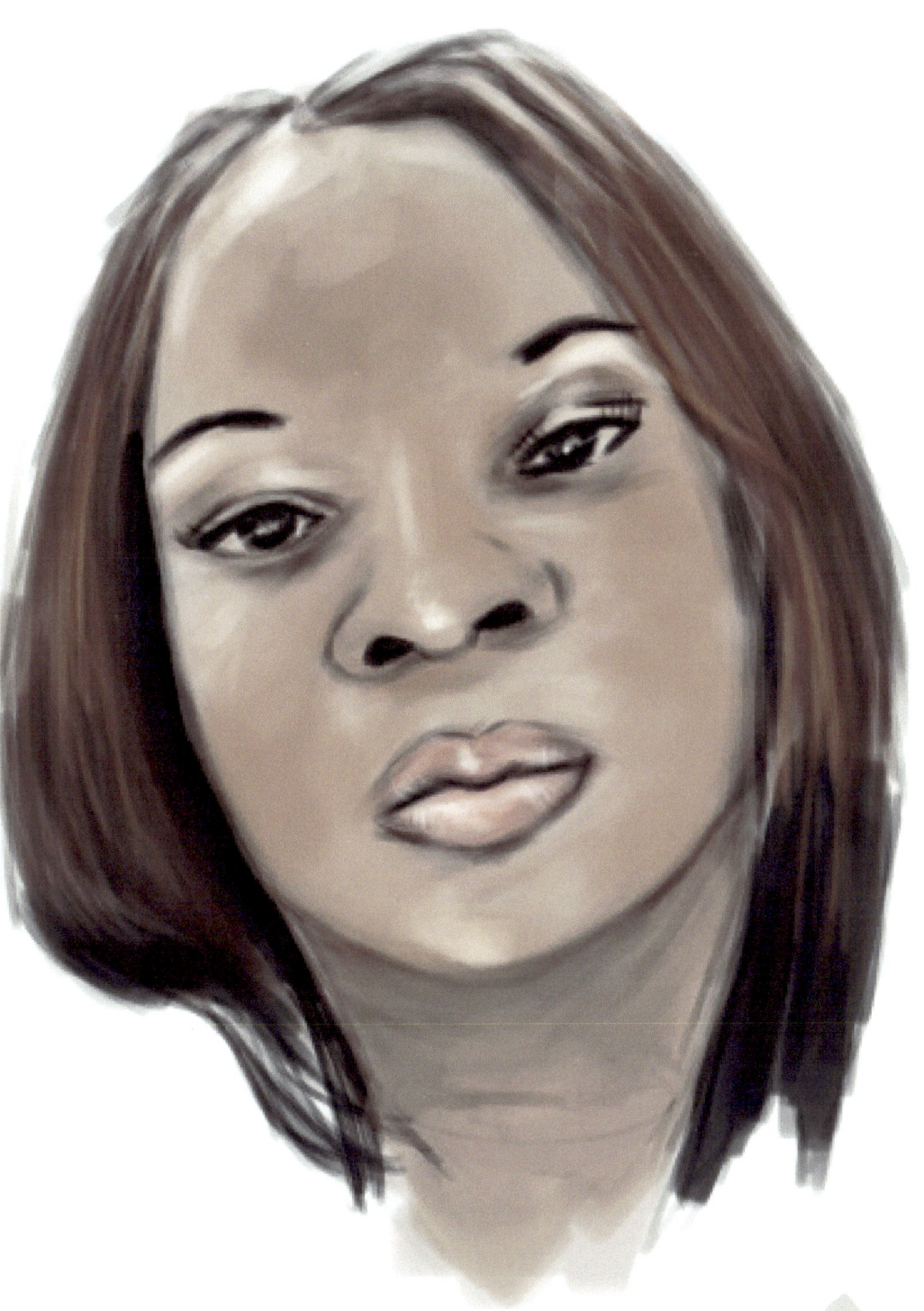

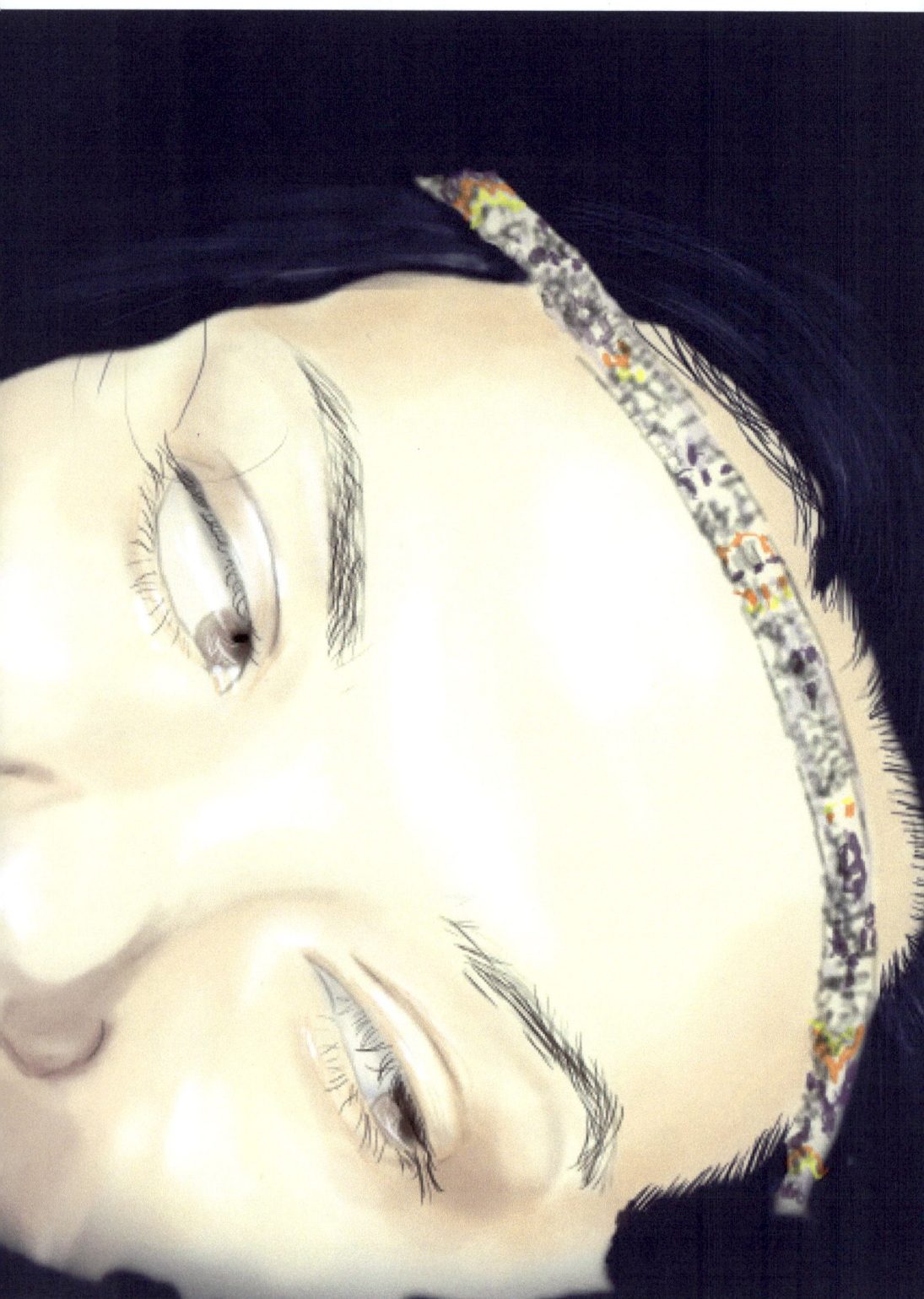

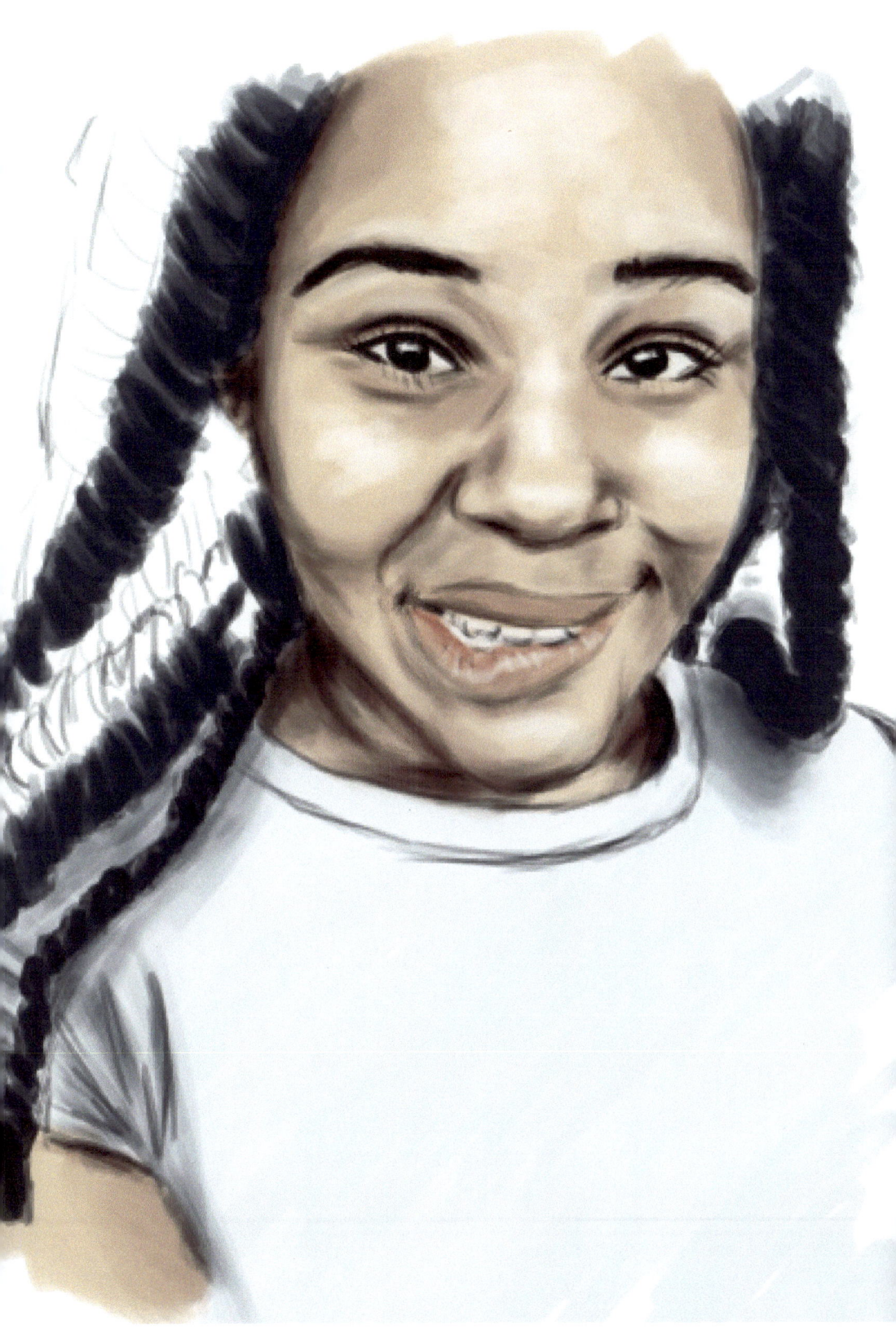

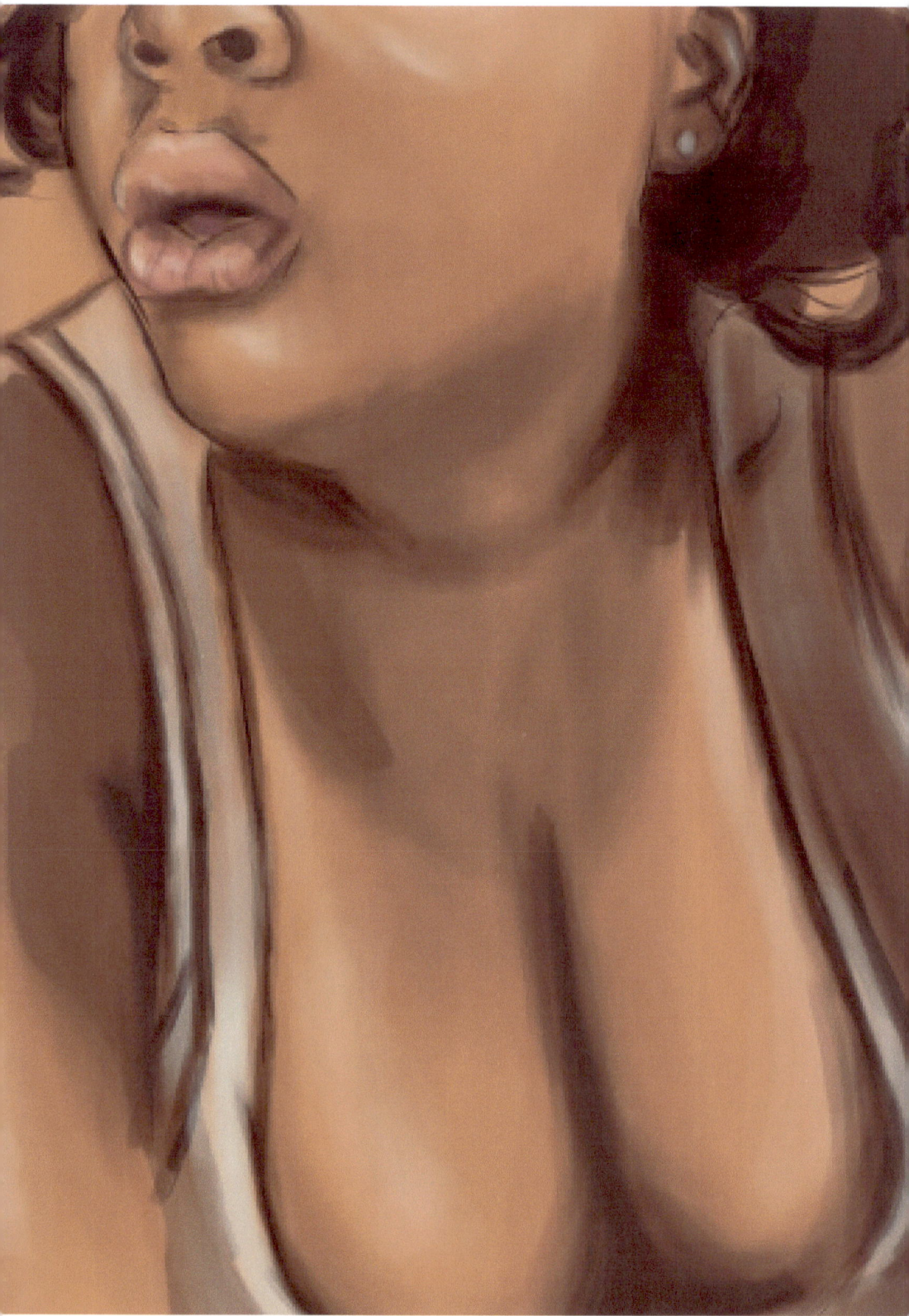

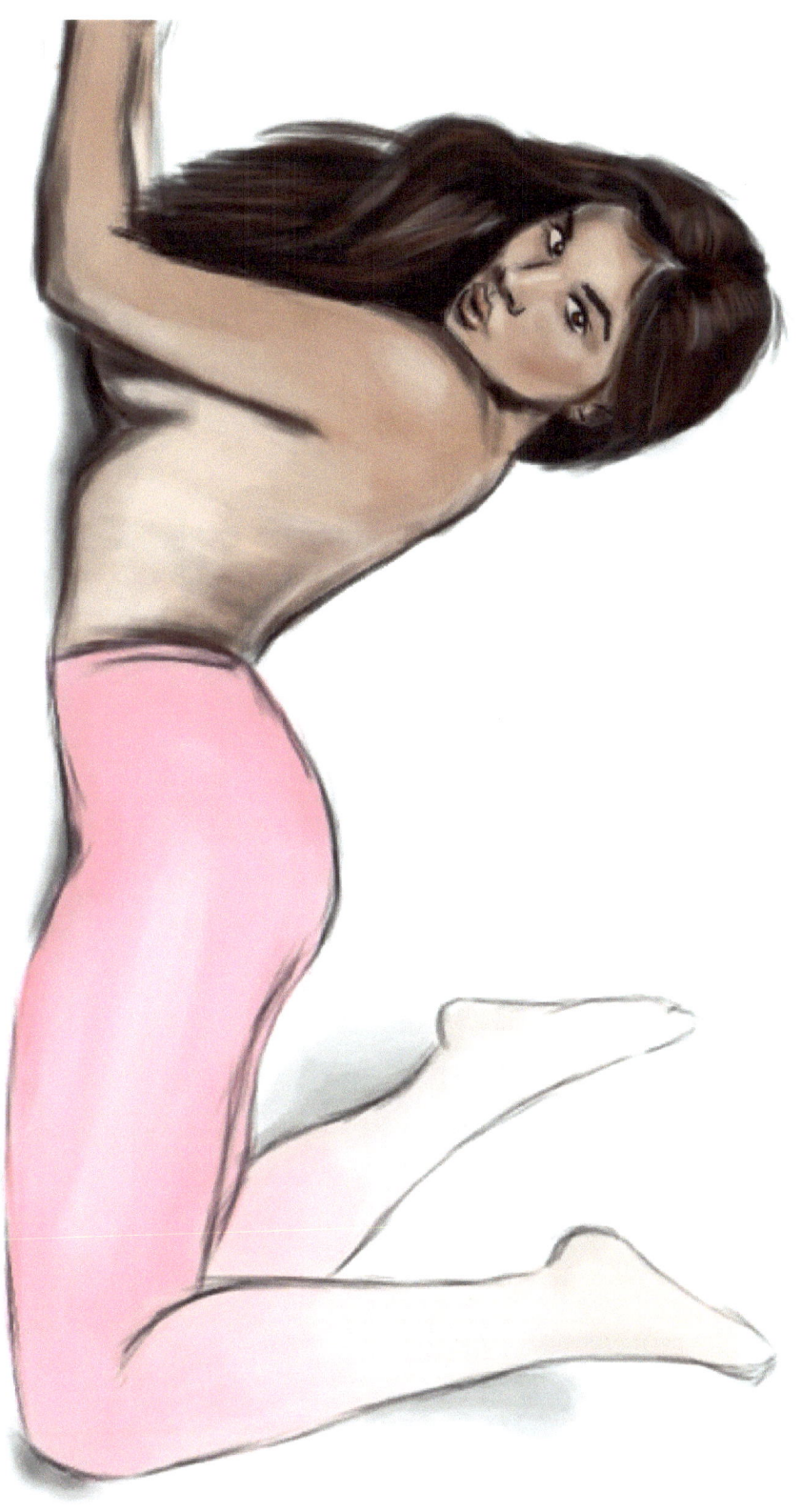

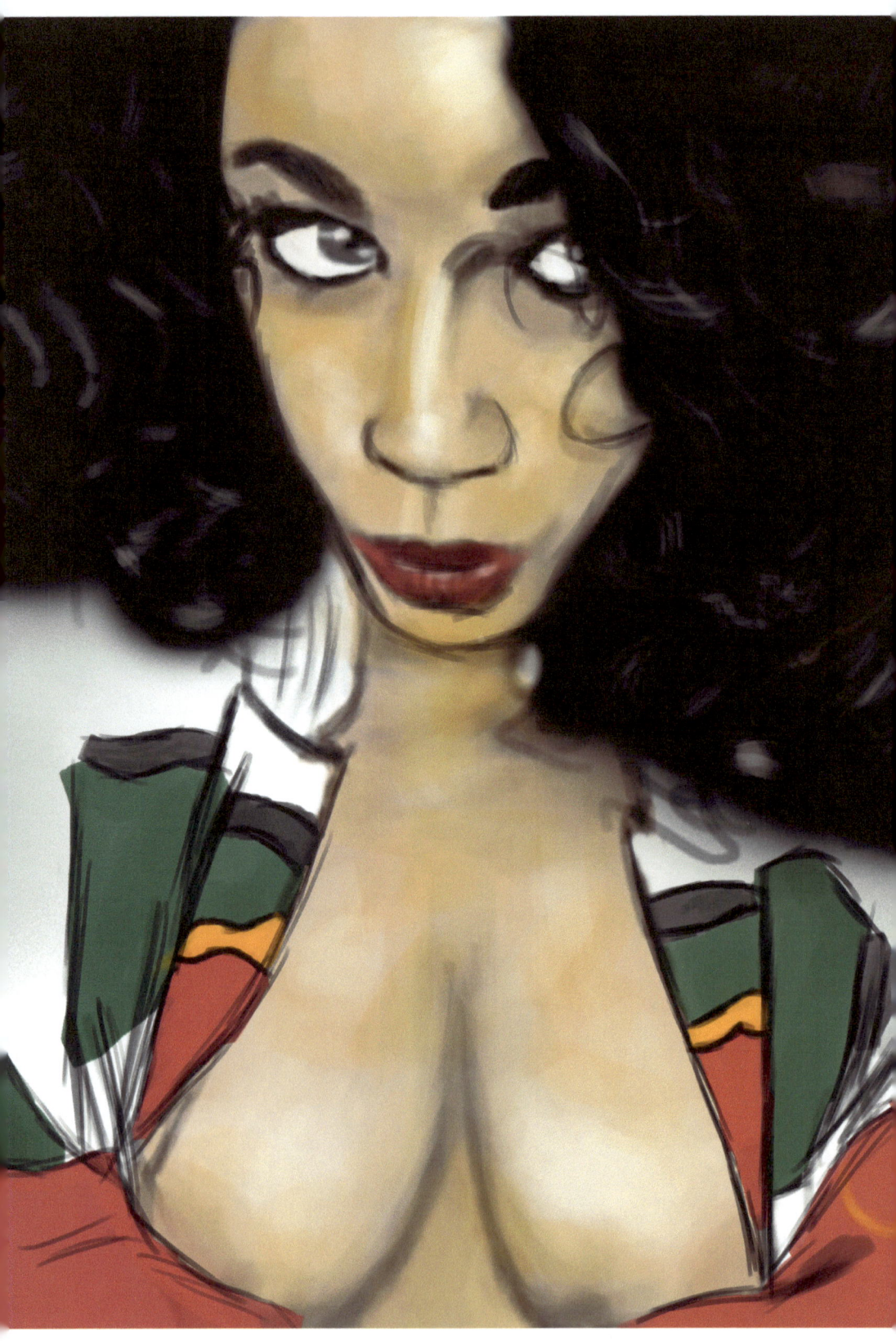

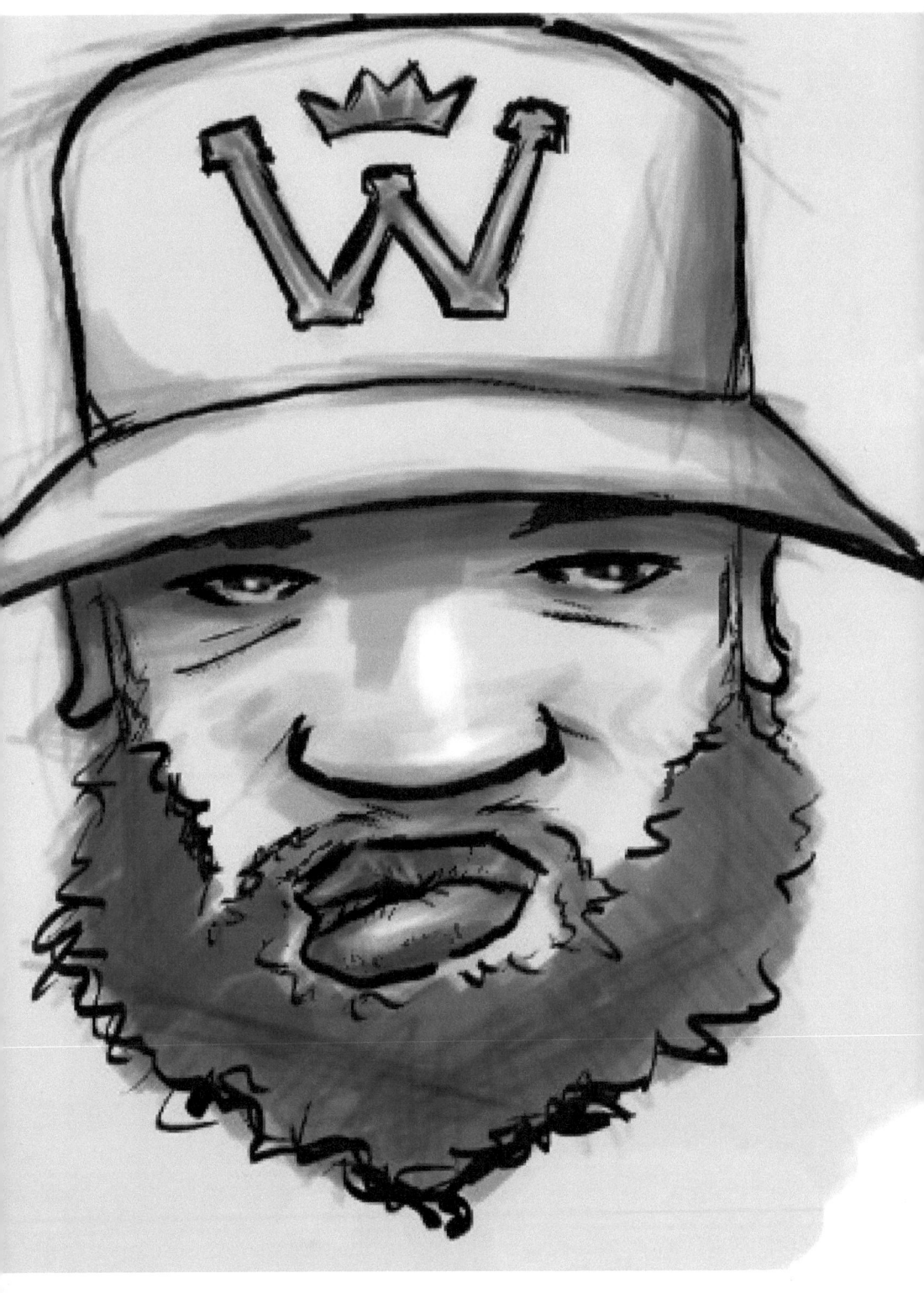

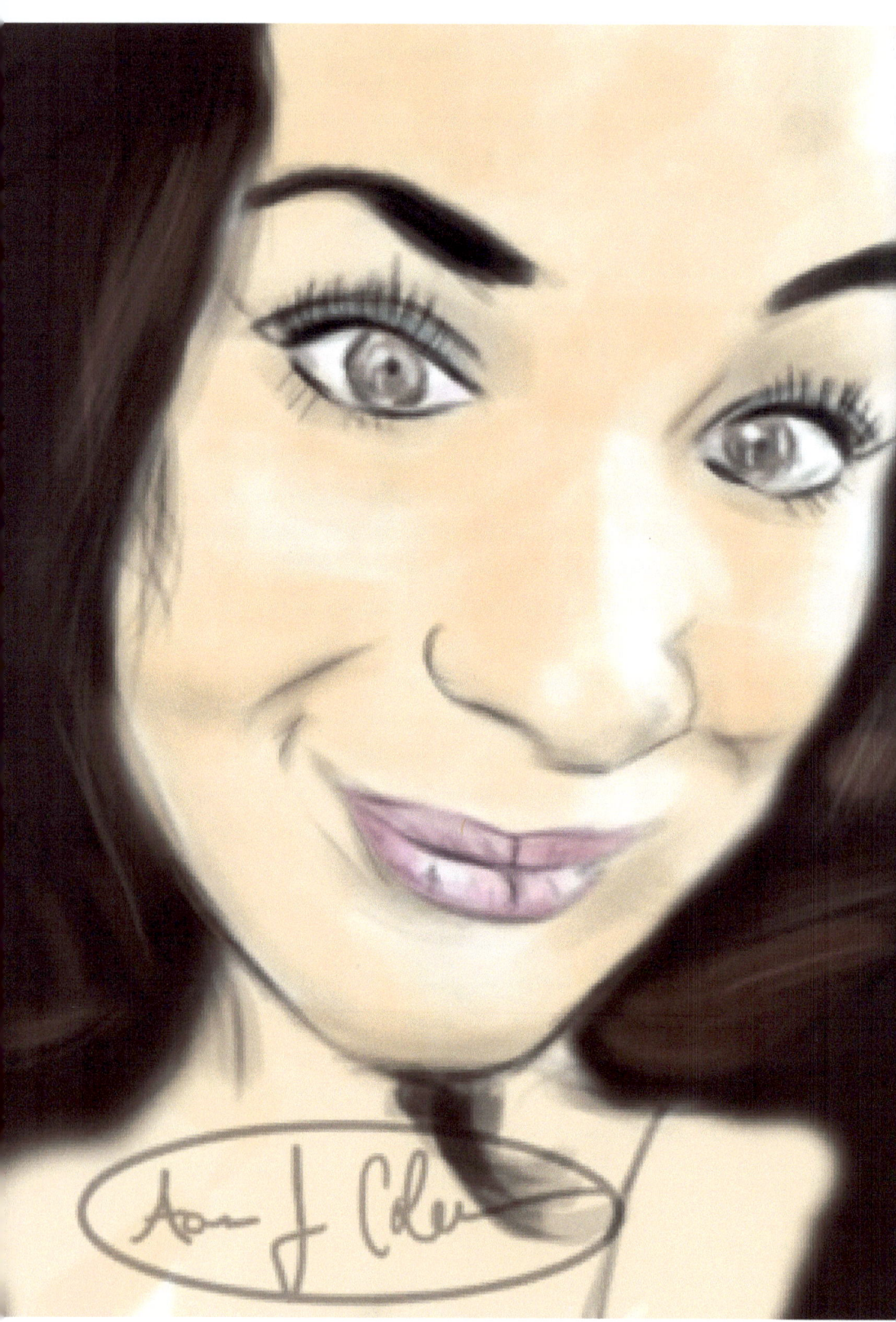

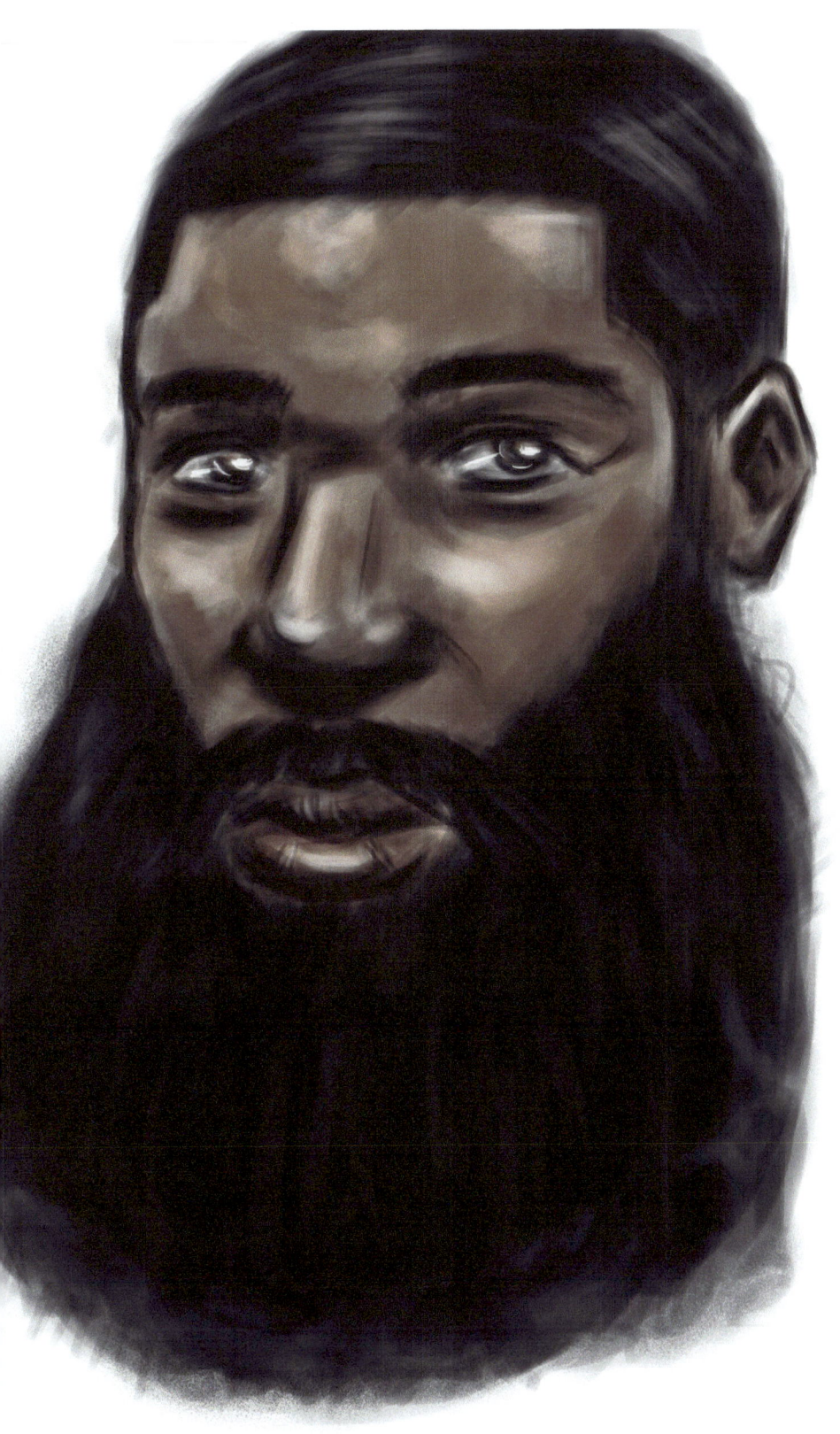

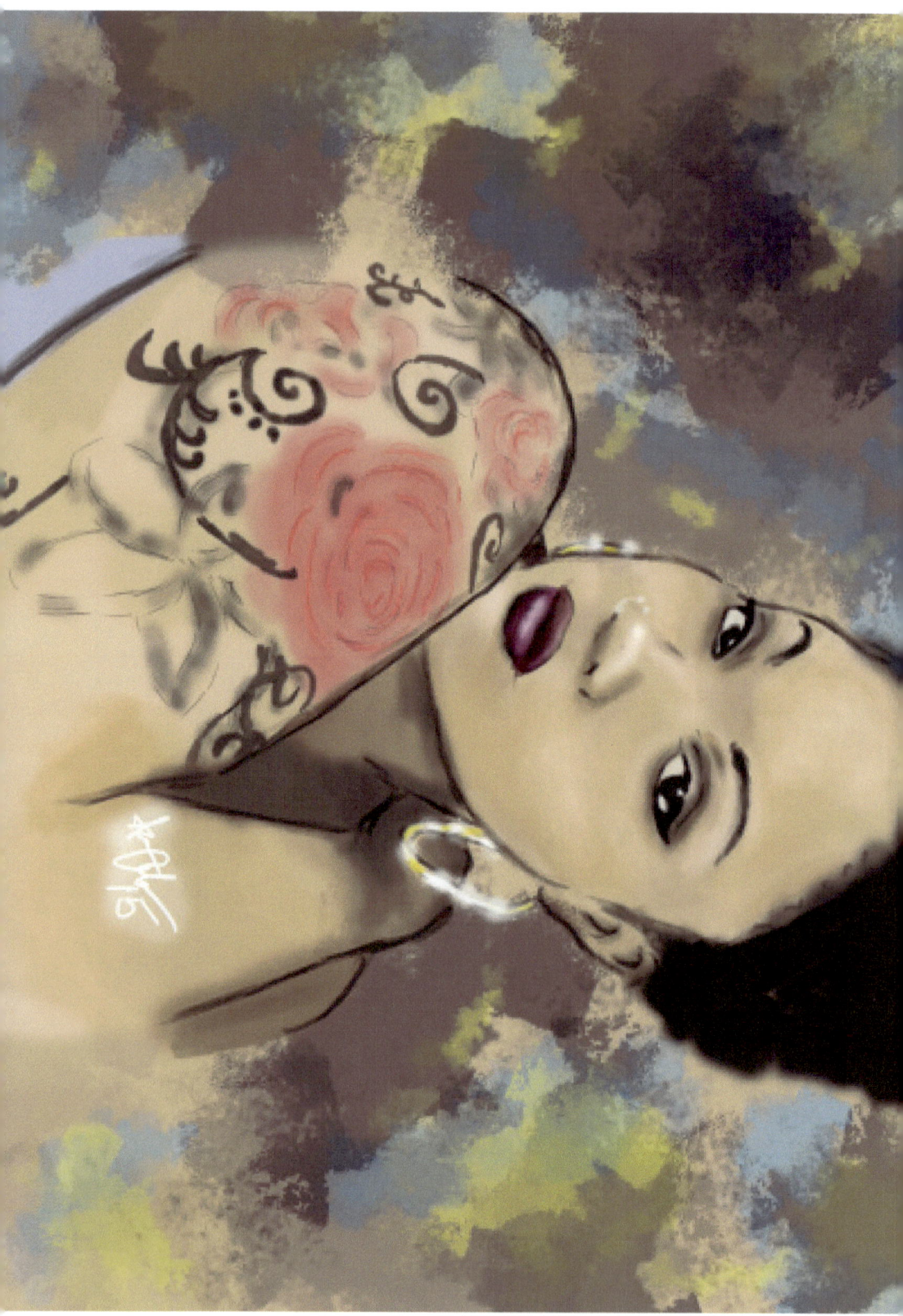

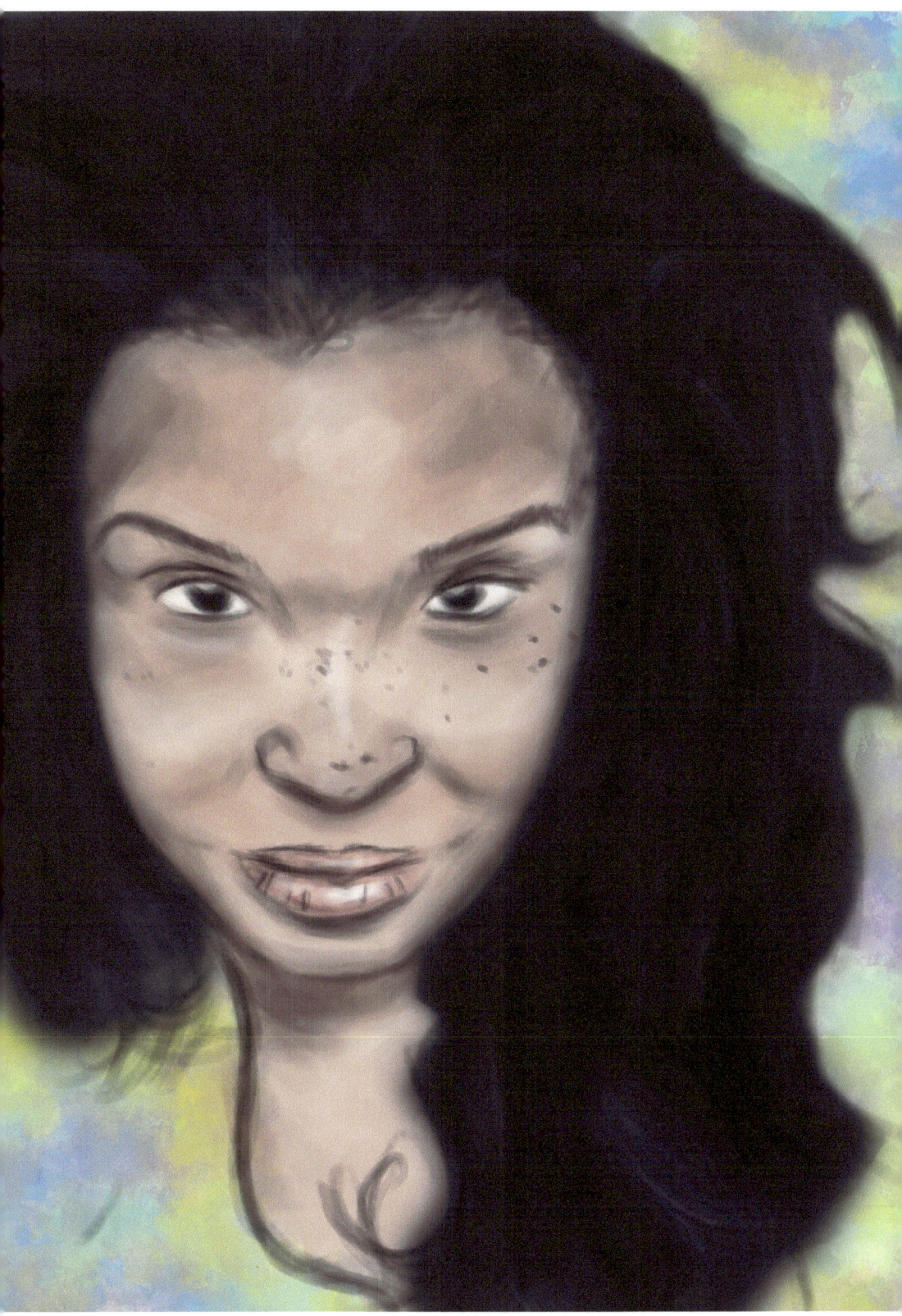

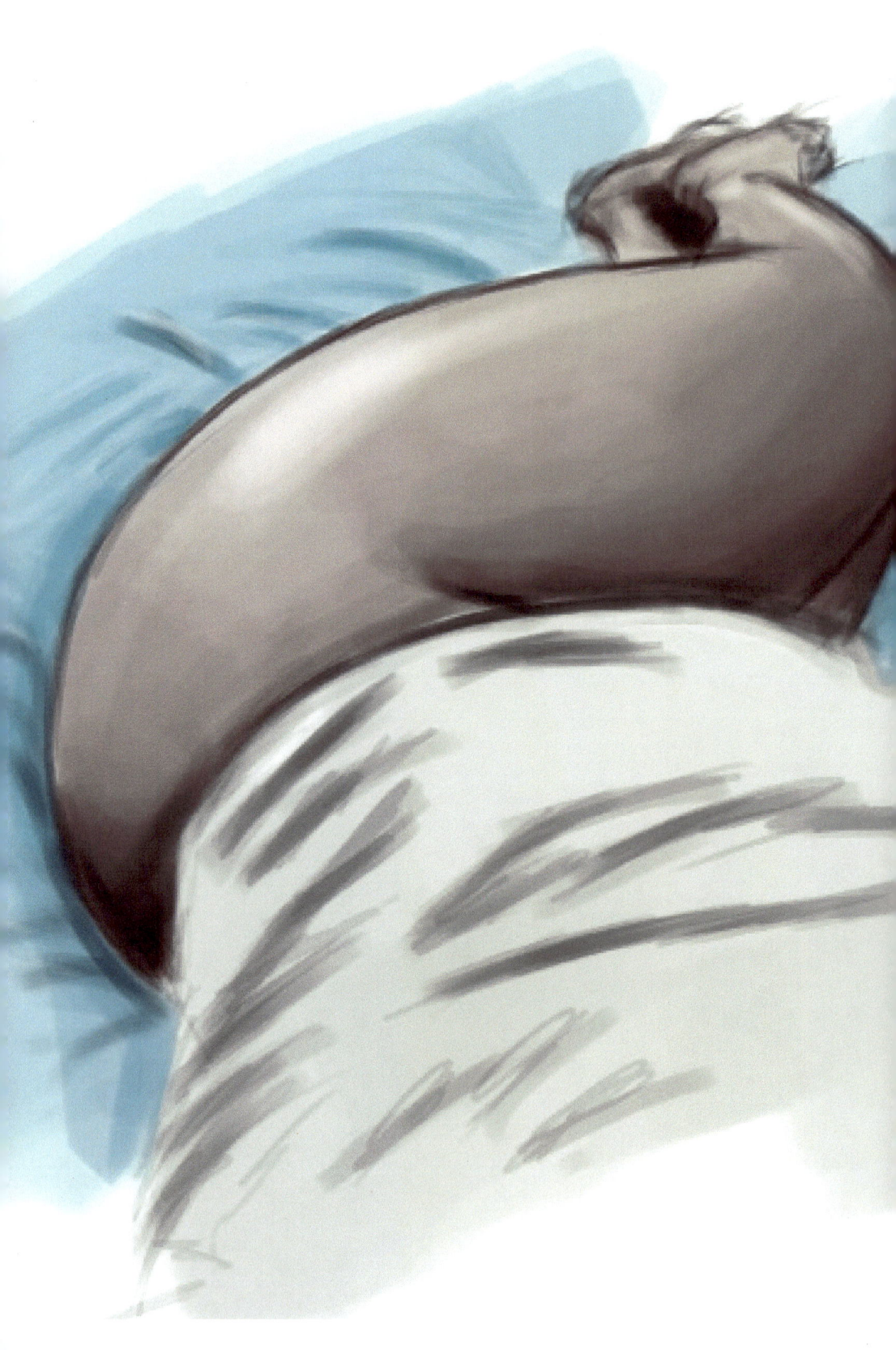

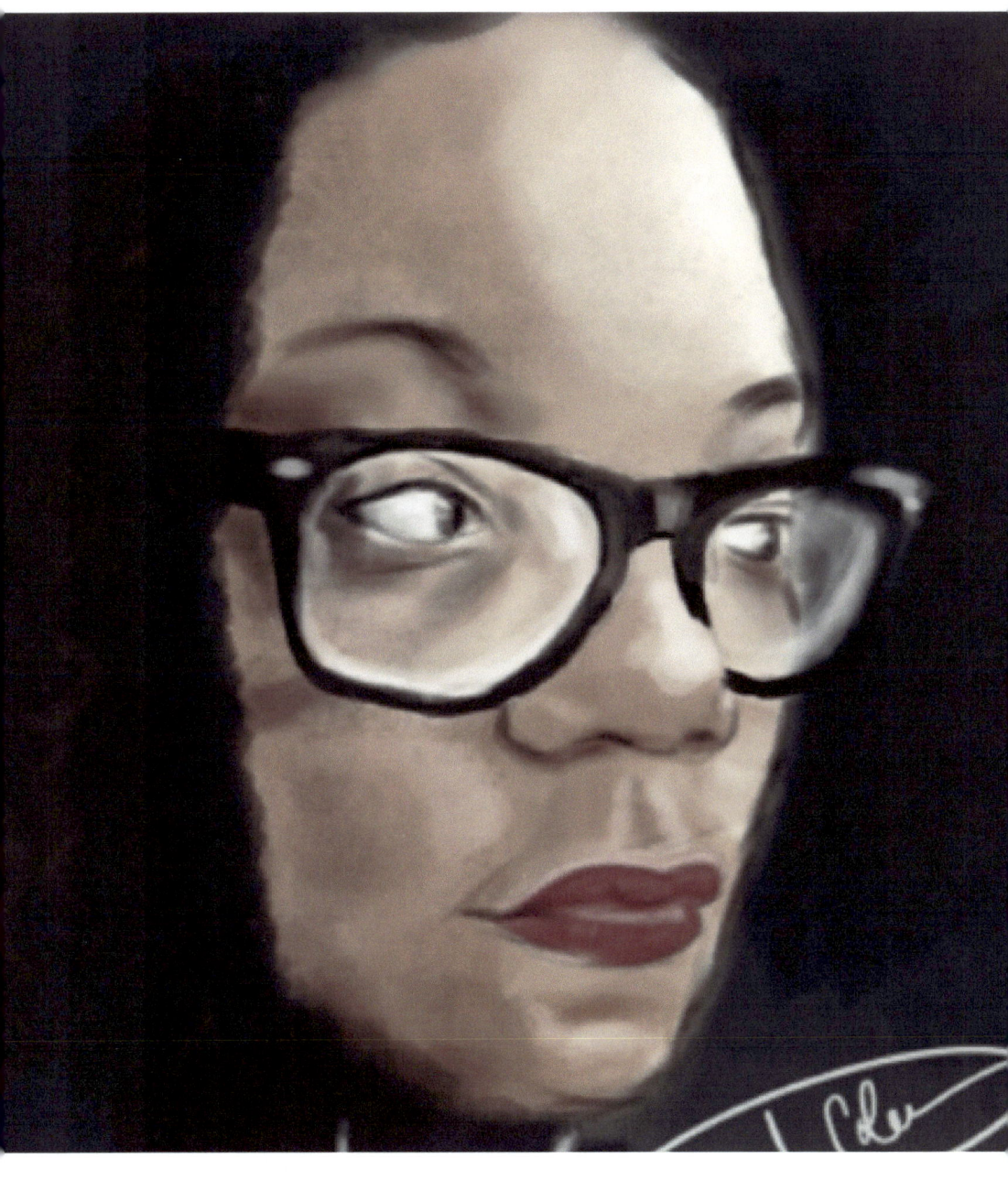

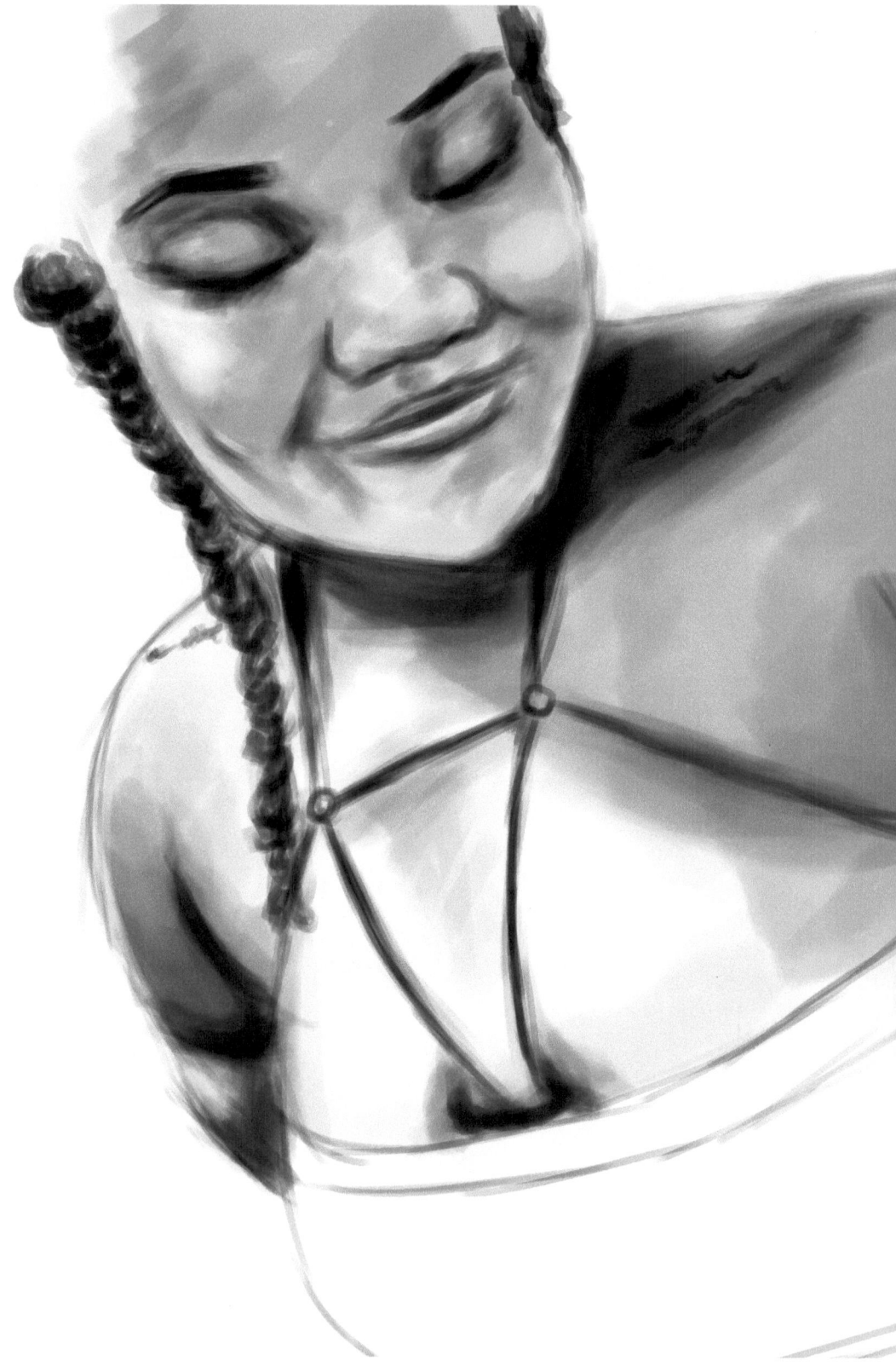

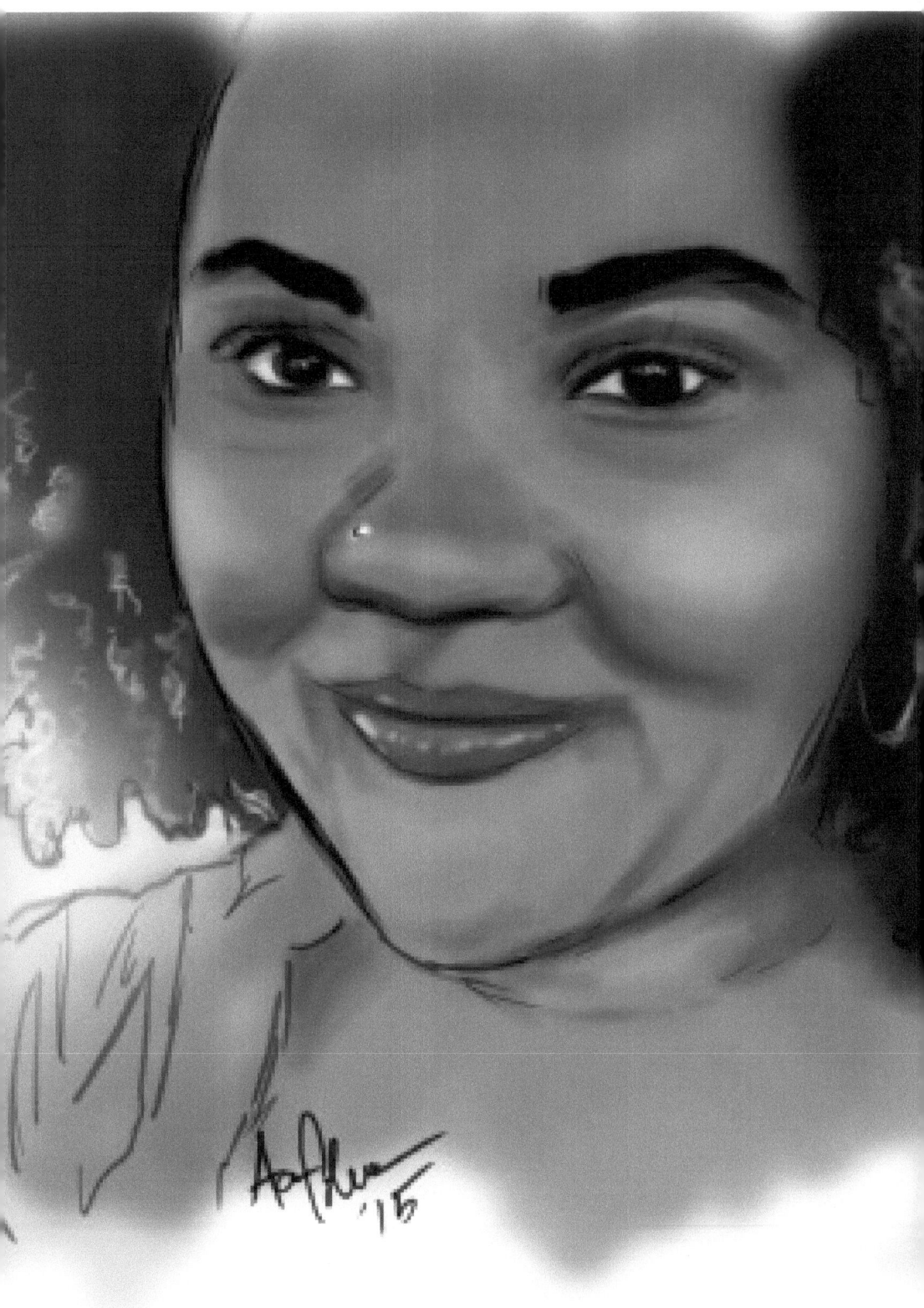

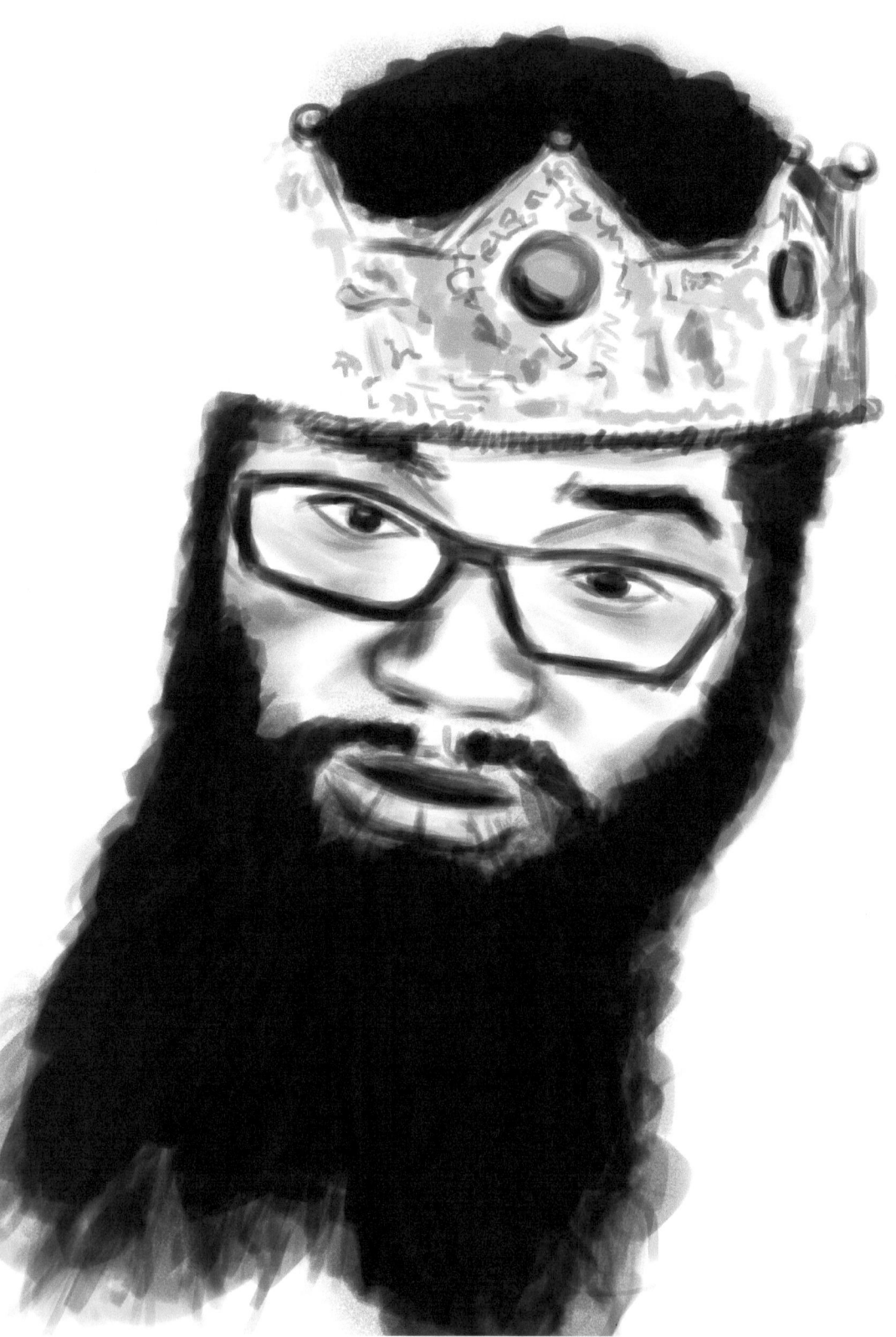

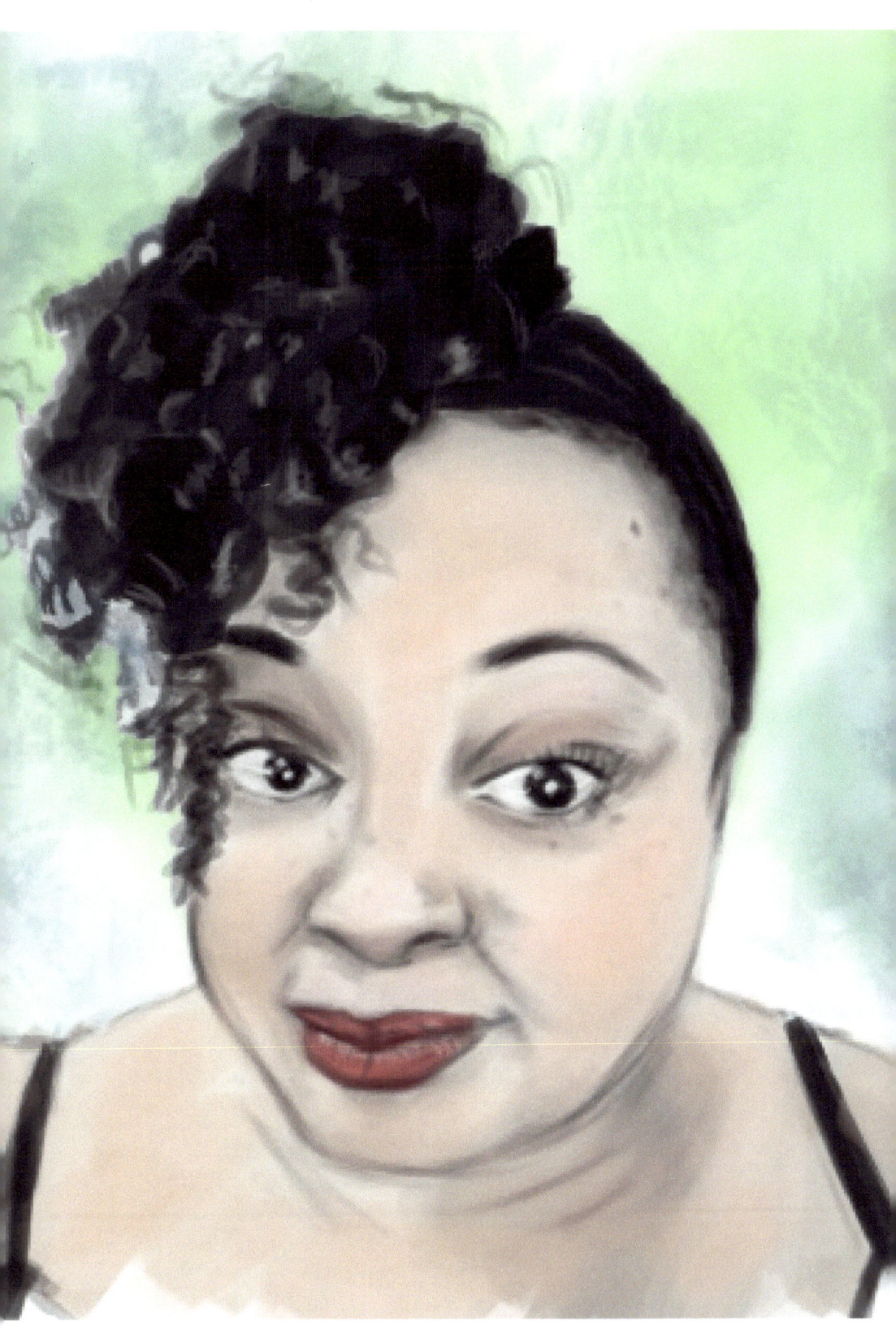

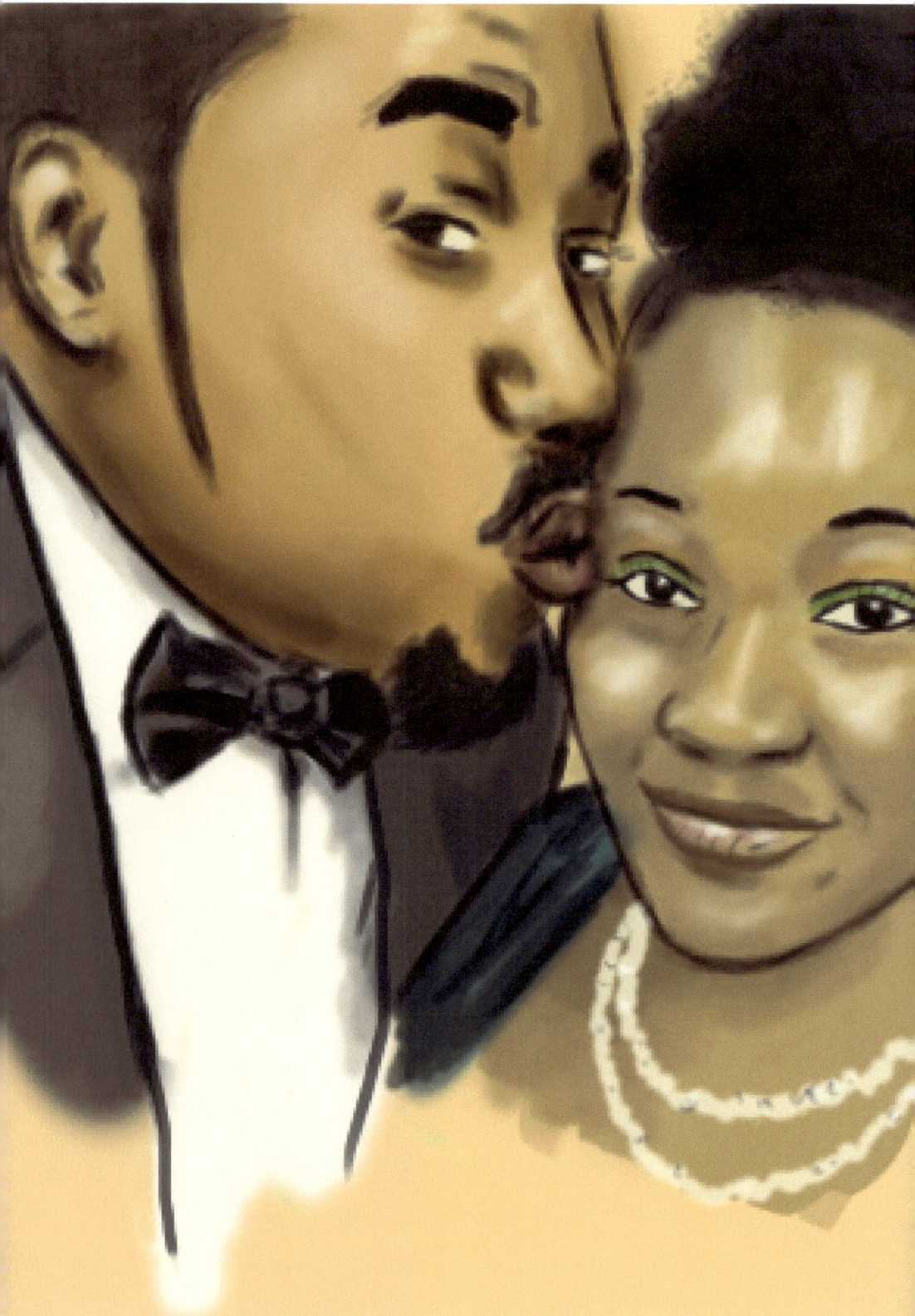

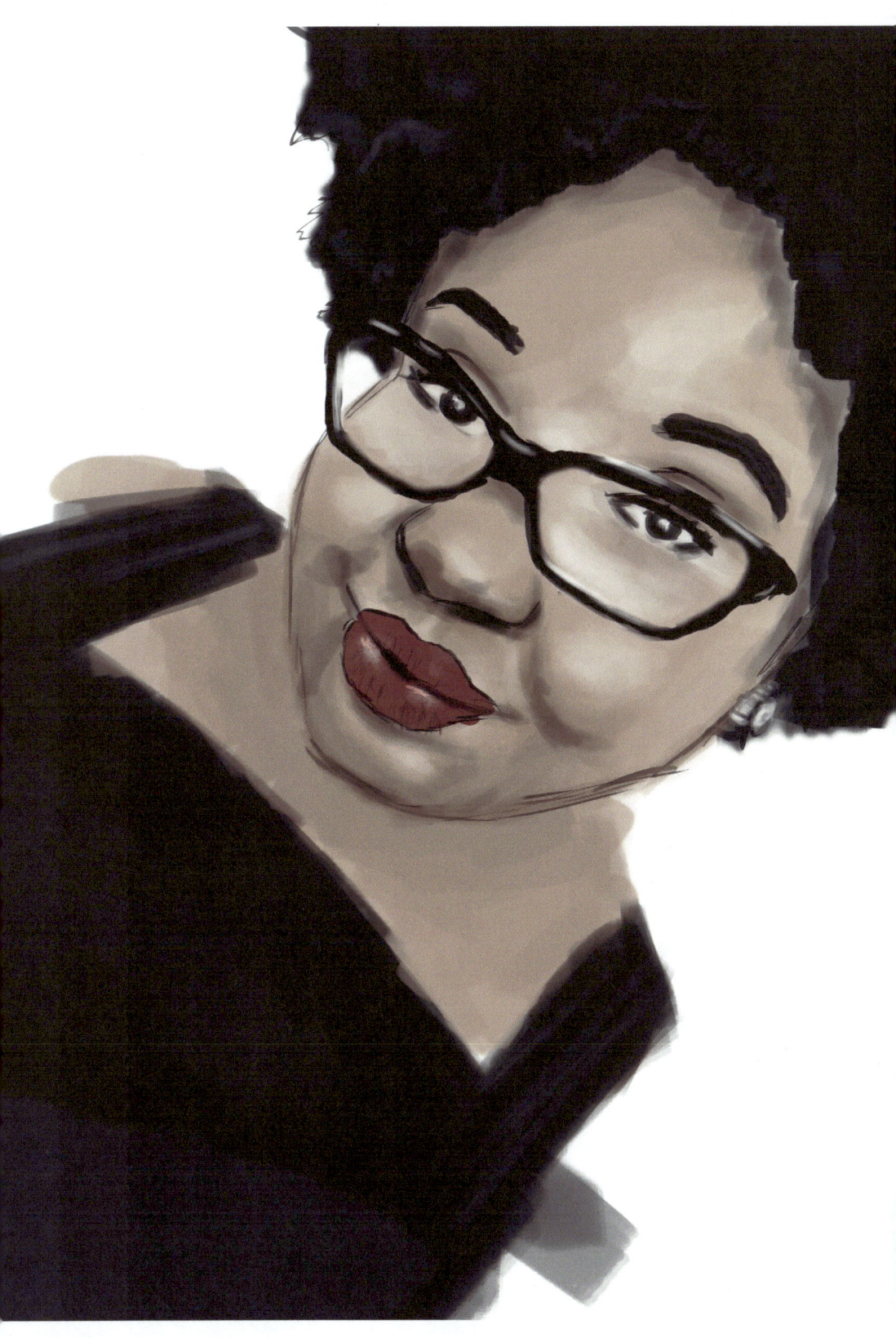

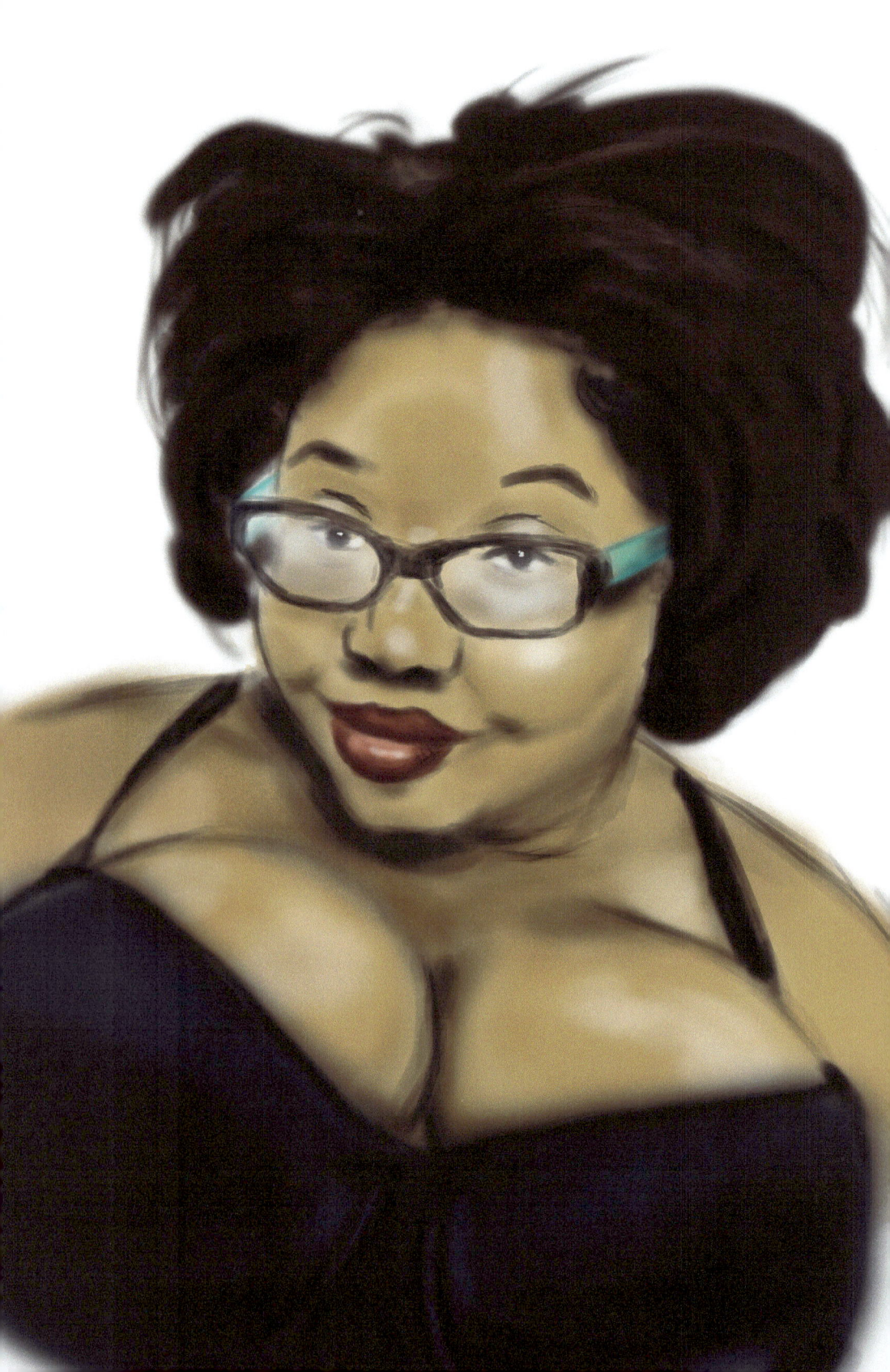

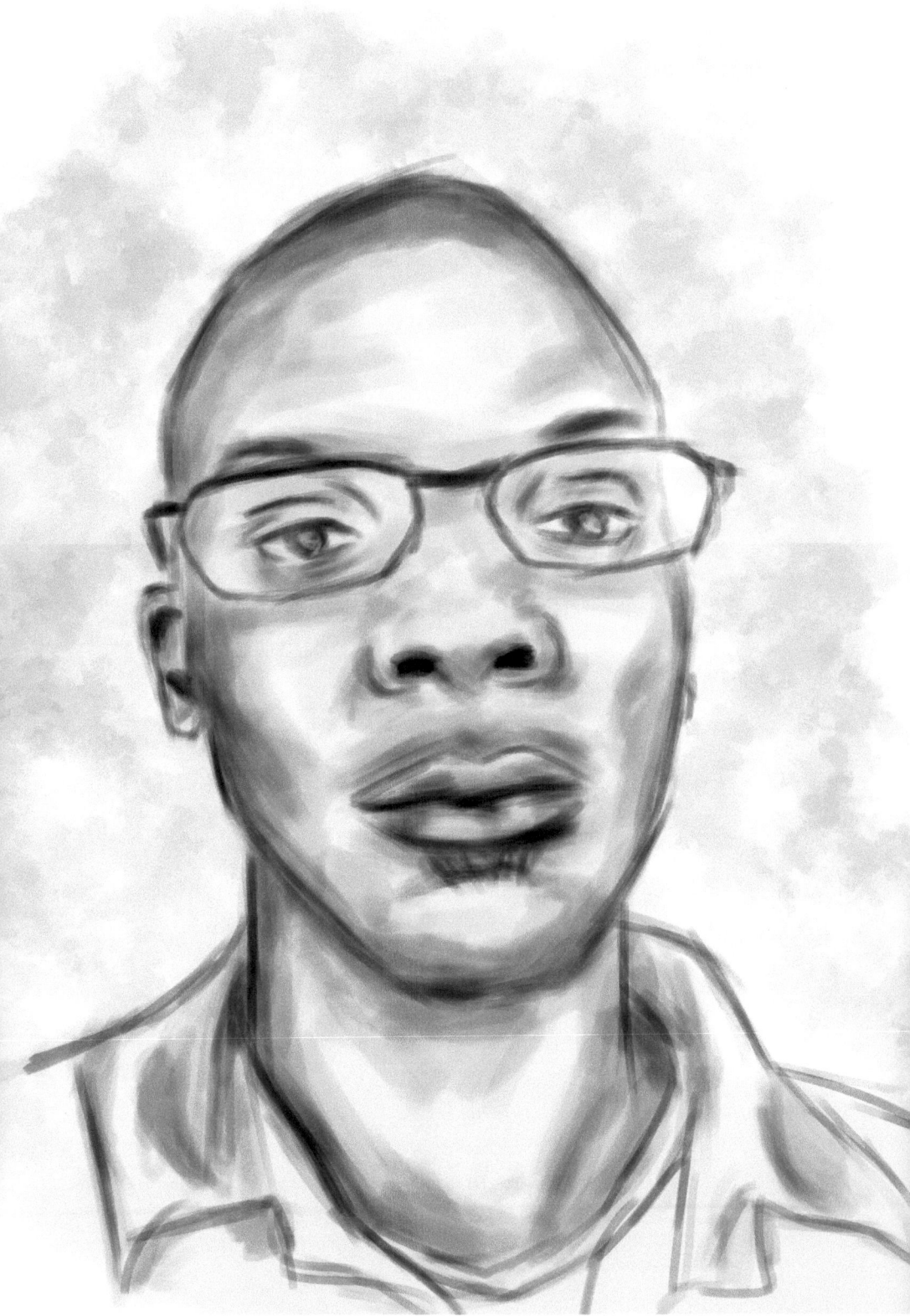

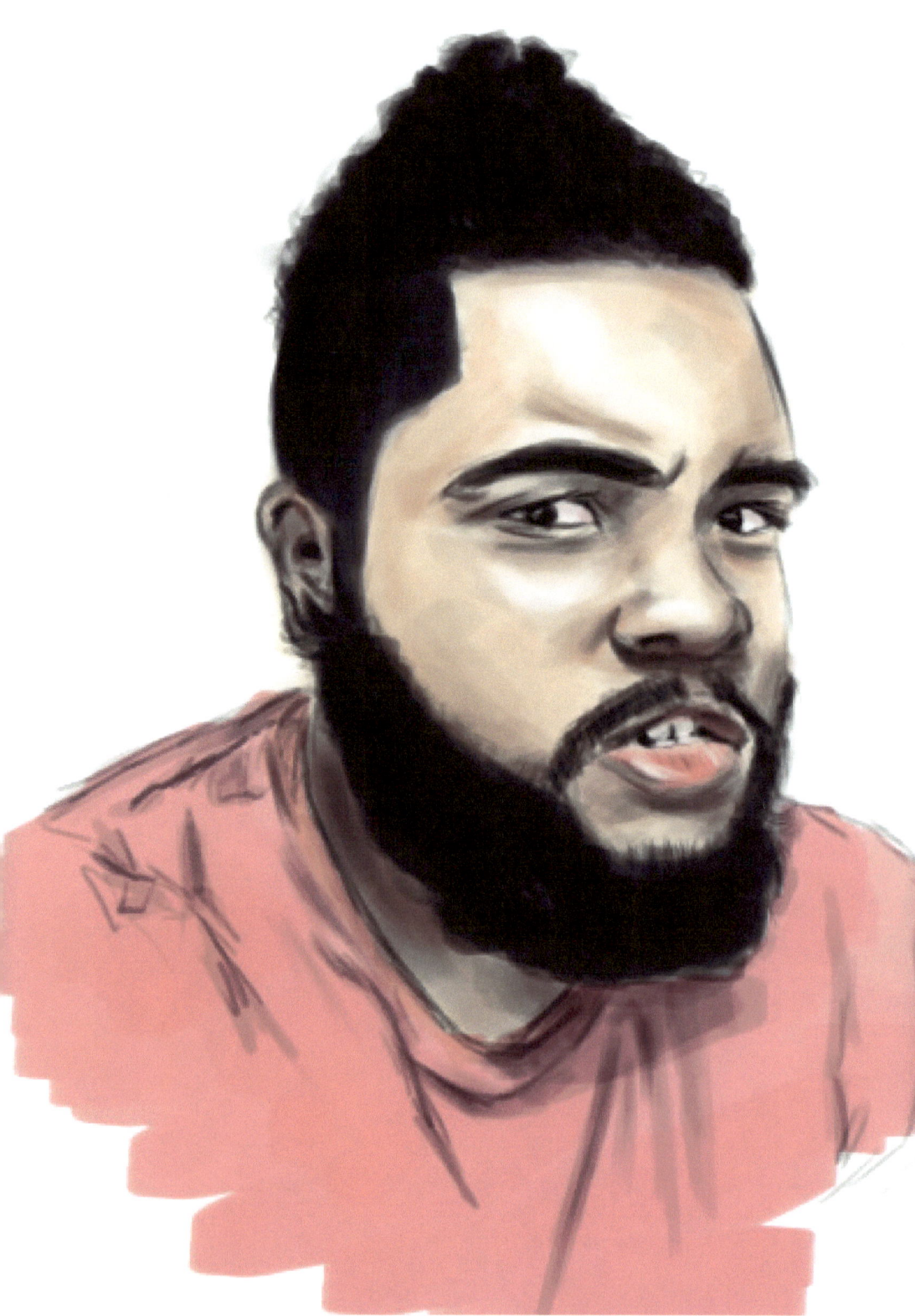

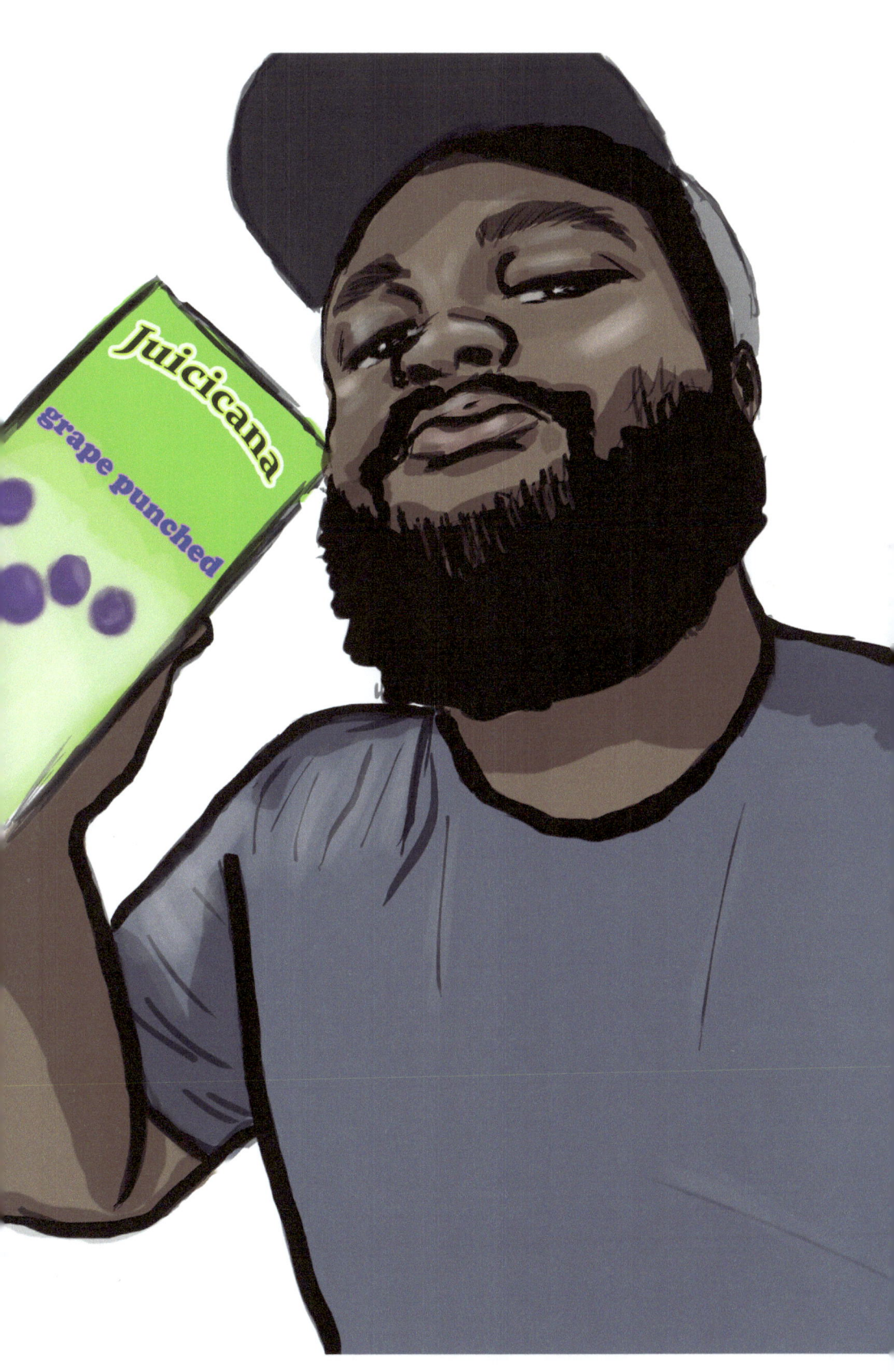

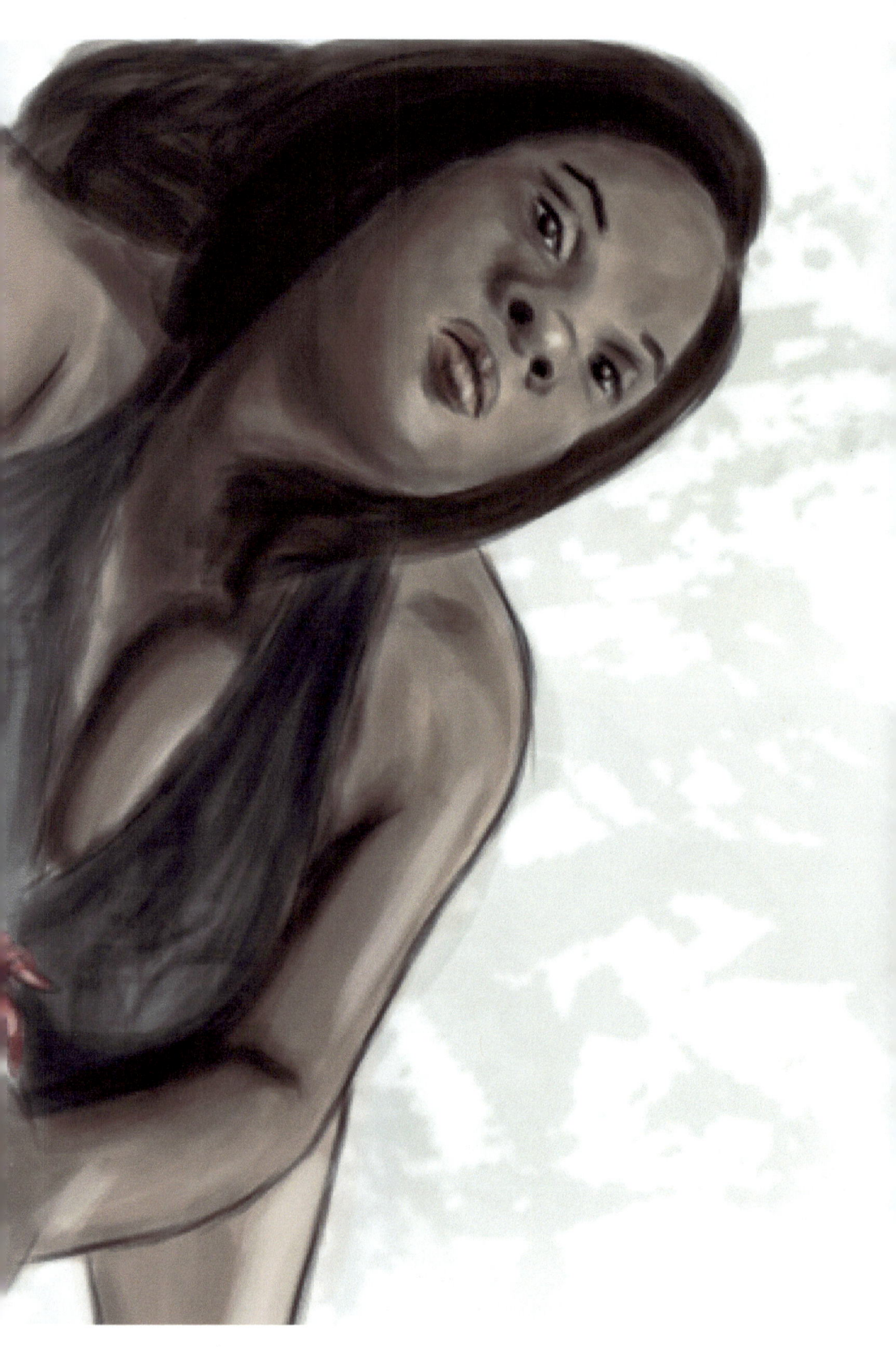

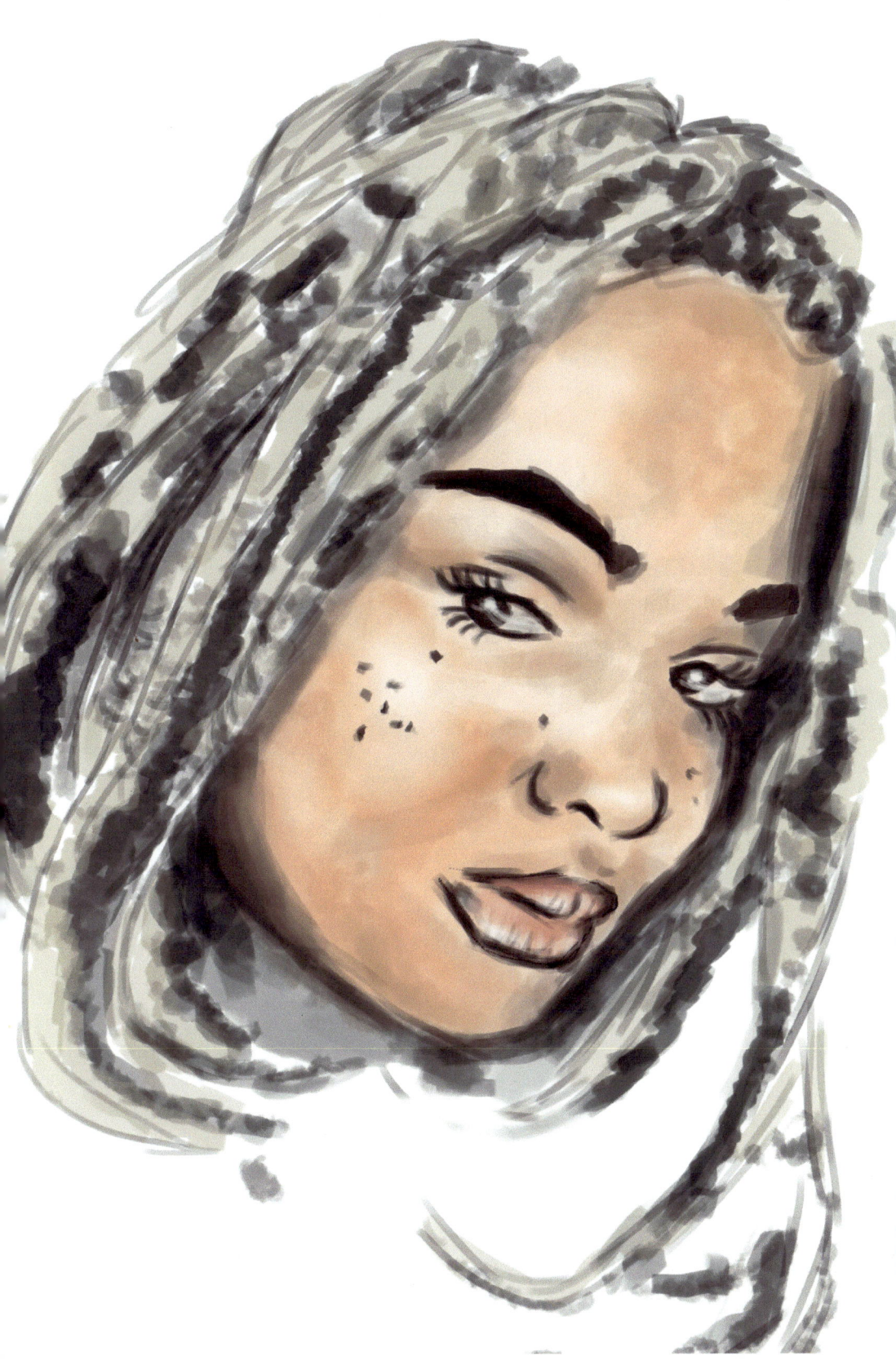

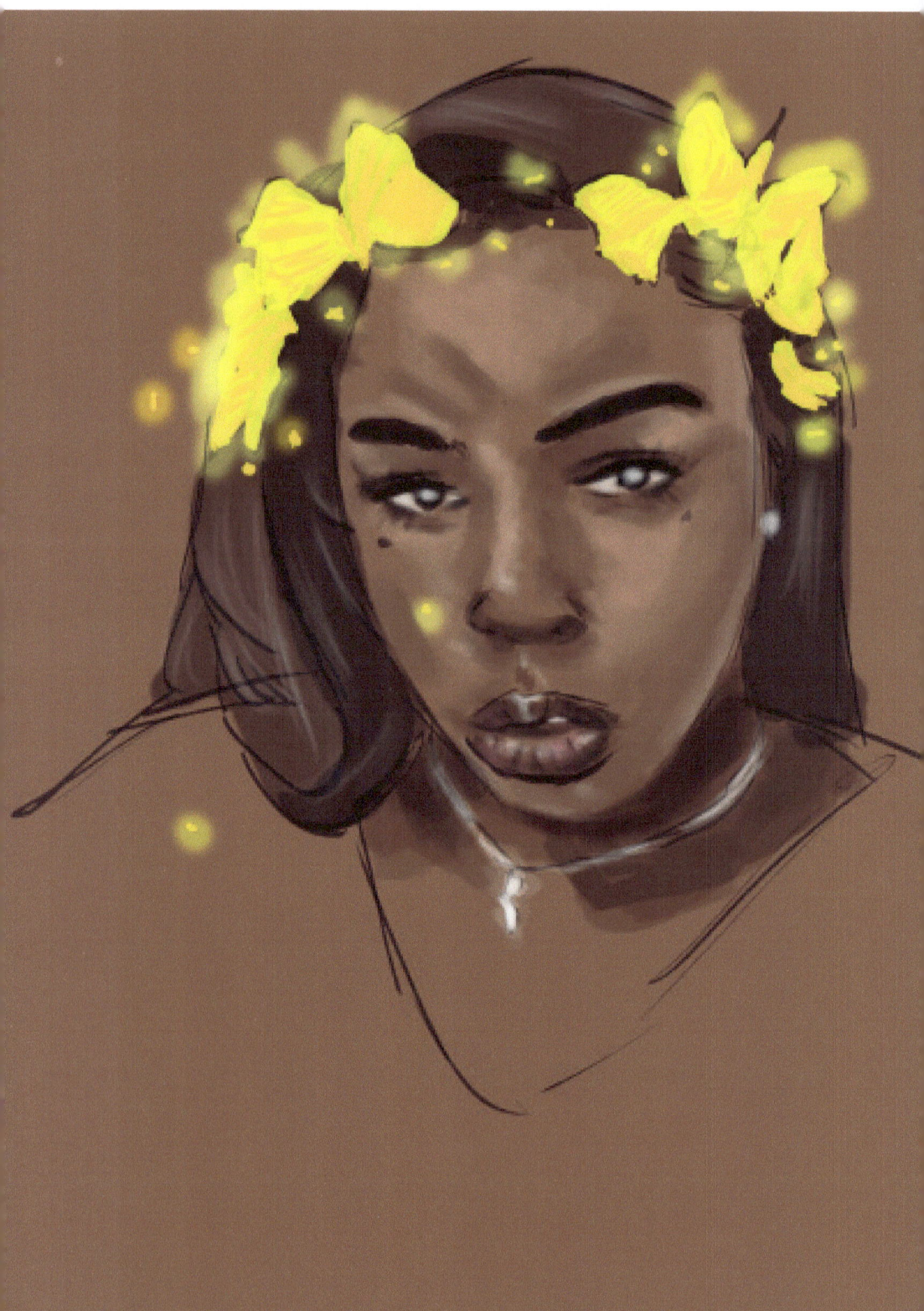

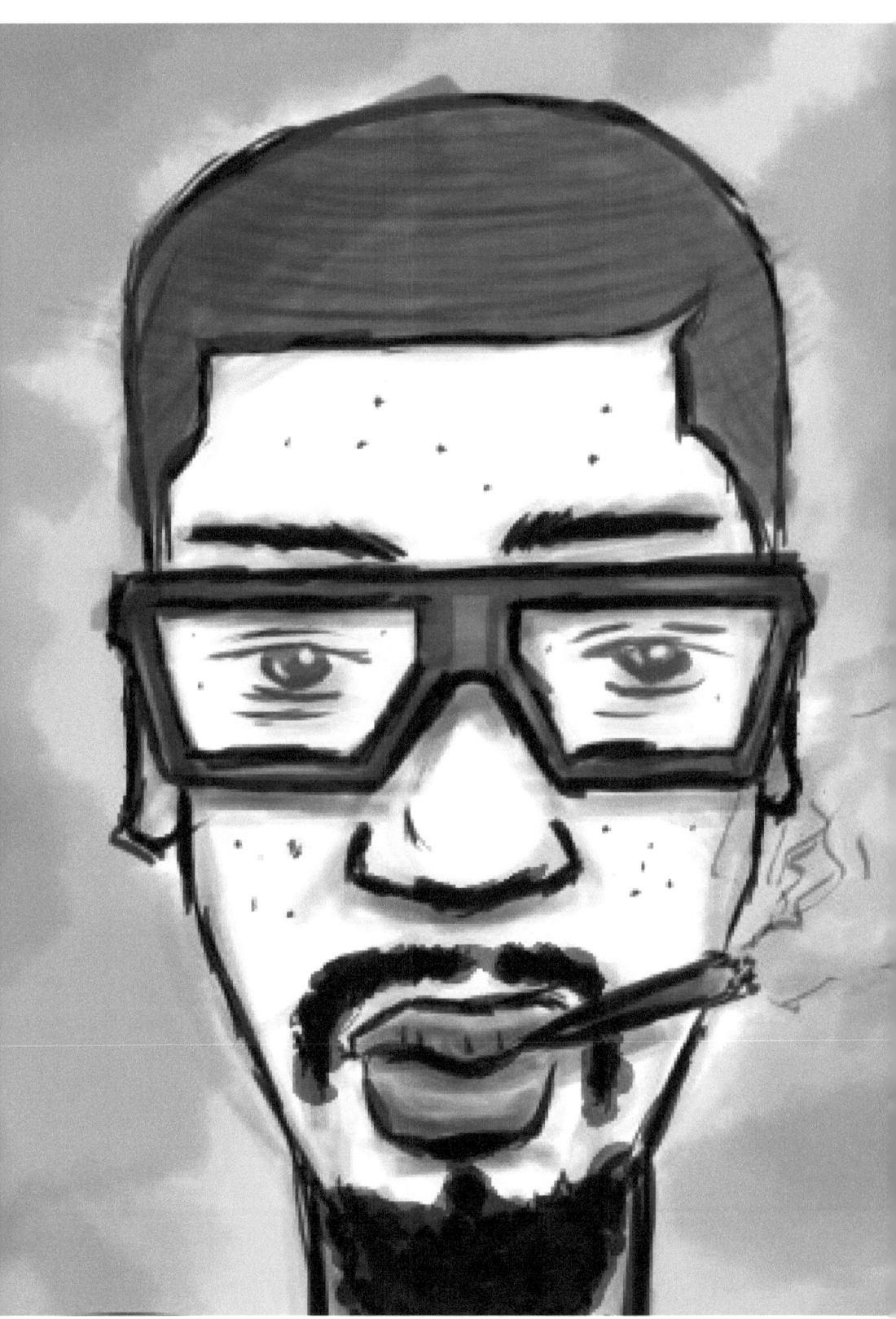

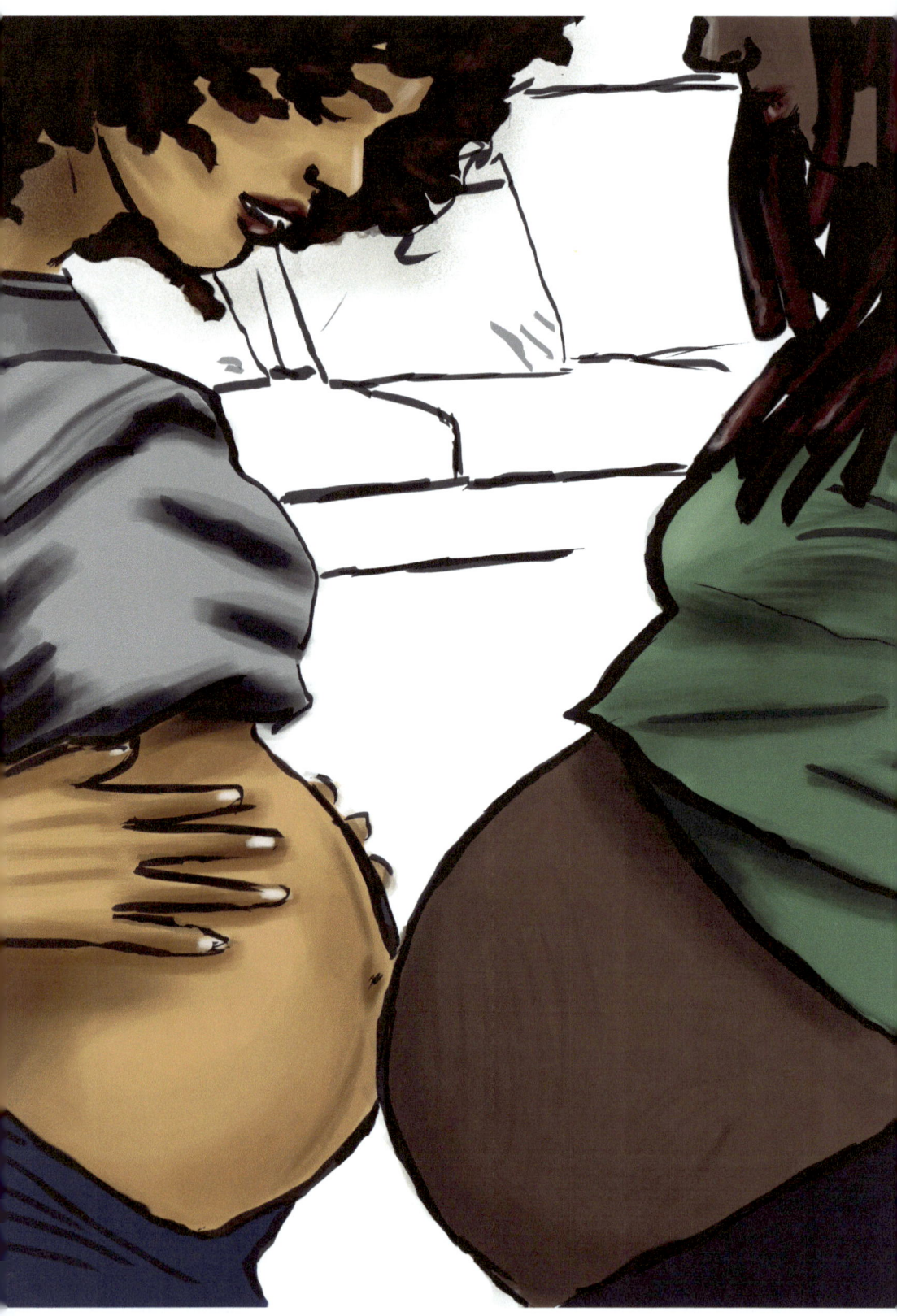

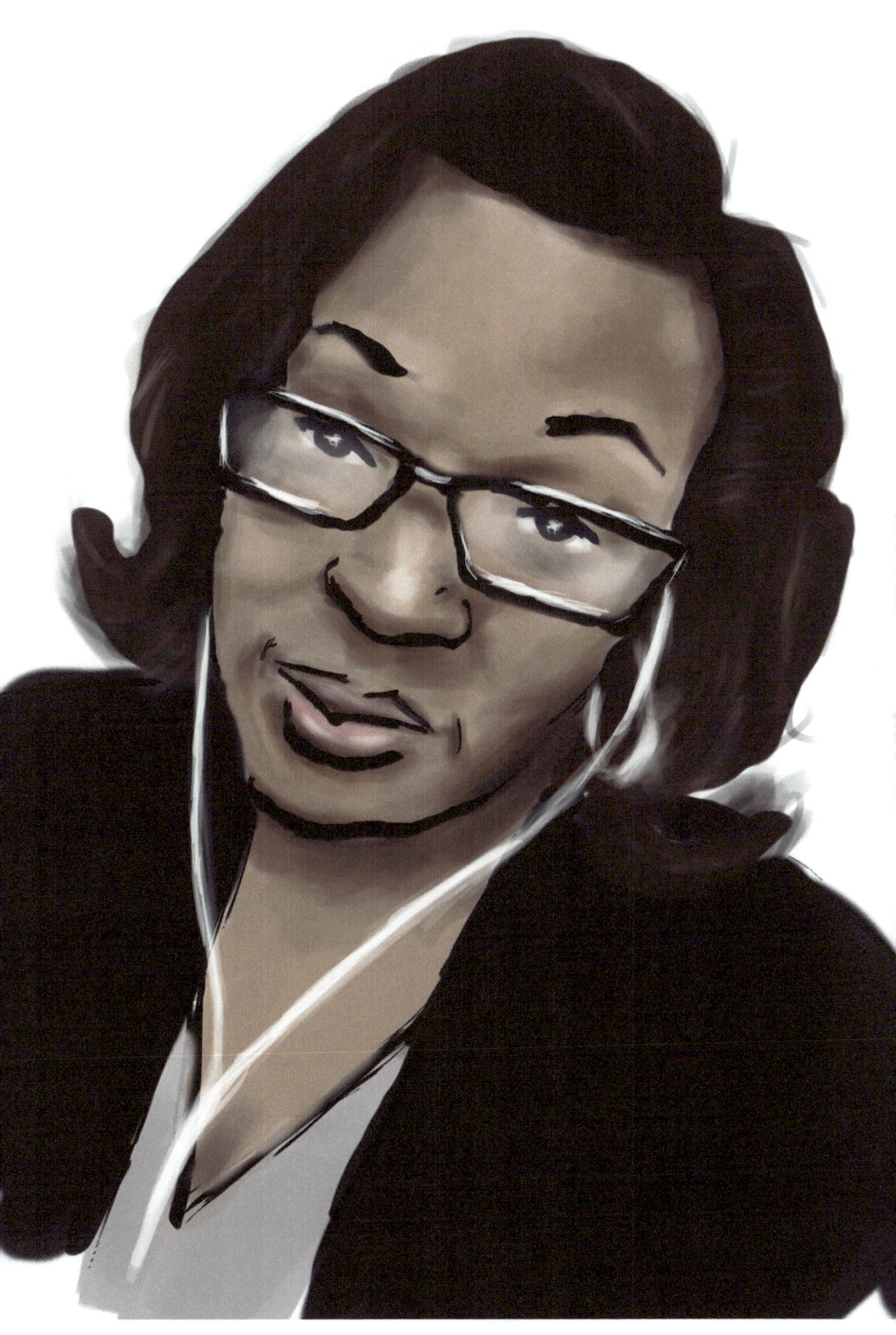

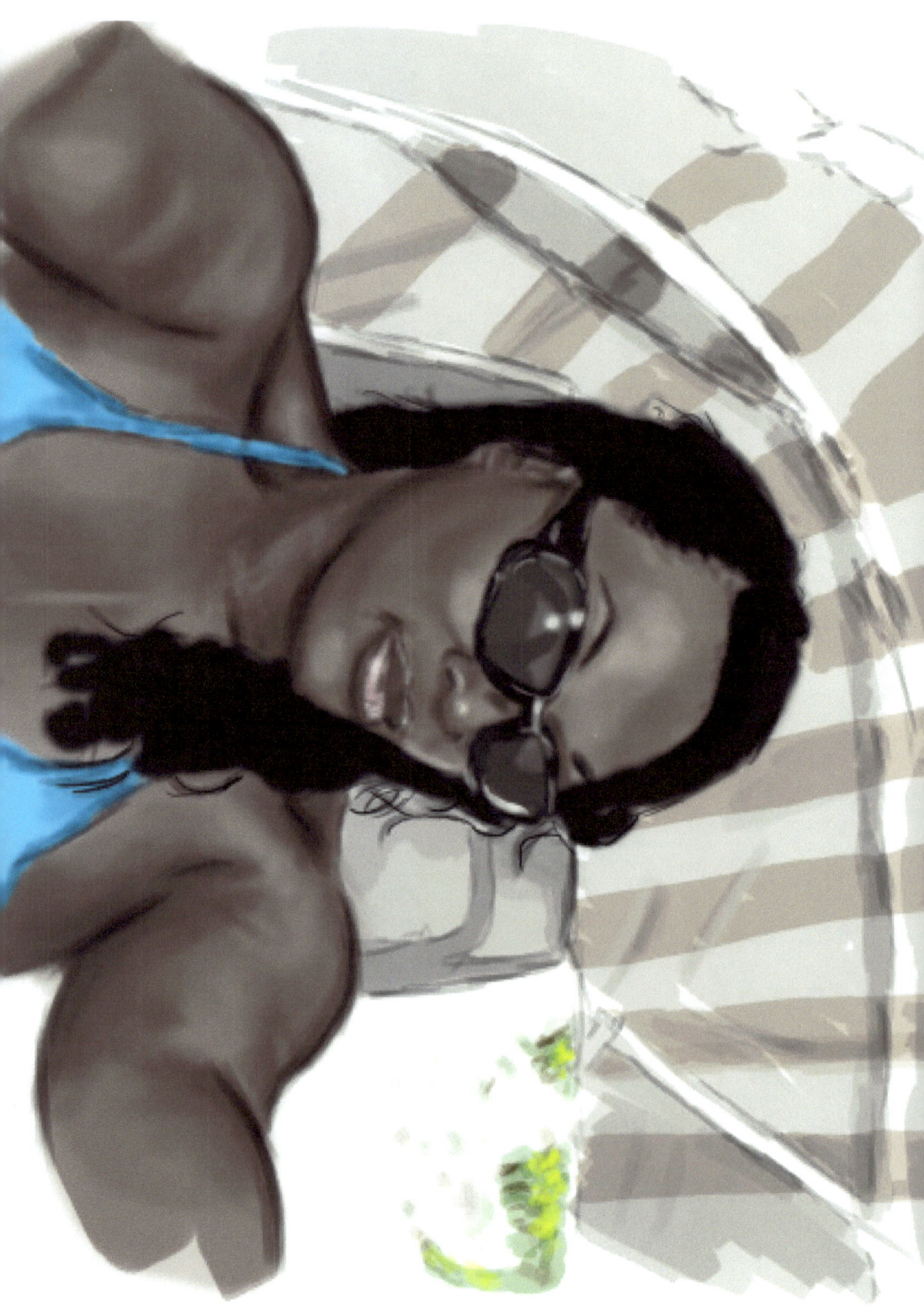

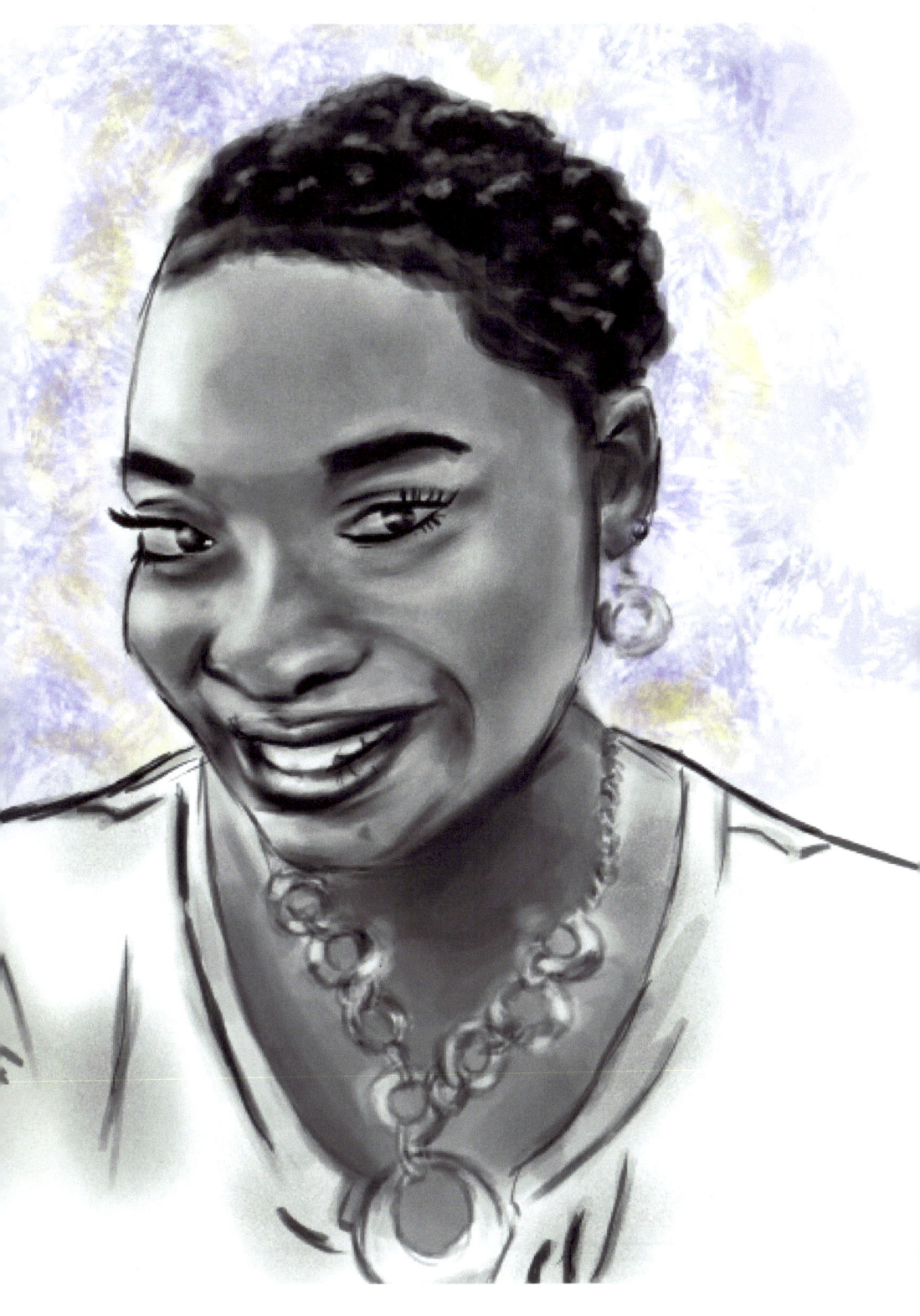

Dedicated to Mom & Da